General Instructior

Materials

All projects are stitched on 7-count plastic canvas, using a #16 tapestry needle and 4-ply worsted weight yarn. Some designs also use metallic craft cord.

Coaster Holders

All pieces for the coaster holders are cut from clear plastic canvas. The graphs for each coaster holder include a bottom and two supports, which are left unstitched except for Whipstitching and Overcasting.

Coasters

Coaster fronts are cut from clear plastic canvas. Coaster backs are matching shapes cut from a complementary color of plastic canvas and are left unstitched.

Stitching

The graphs for the coaster holder bottoms and some other graphs are marked with colored lines that indicate where pieces are Whipstitched together. Leave these lines unworked as you complete any surrounding background stitches; they will be stitched when the piece is assembled.

Once th
Backstitch … embroidery stitches using 2 plies separated from a length of worsted weight yarn, following the color key for the individual design.

Assembly

The left side of each coaster holder has a wide "doorway" where coasters are inserted into the holder for storage. Once all pieces for the coaster holder have been stitched, Whipstitch the front edge of an unstitched support to each side of the doorway. The front edge of each support has a cutout notch. As you Whipstitch each support to the doorway, Overcast the notch in the support and the adjacent edge of the coaster holder's left side.

Next, Whipstitch the bottom edges of the supports to the unstitched coaster holder bottom where indicated by the colored lines on the graph. Overcast all remaining edges of the supports.

Continue with assembly as described in the instructions for each design.

Pet Shop

Size: **Coaster Holder:** 6¼ inches W x 6⅝ inches H x 5⅜ inches D (15.9cm x 16.8cm x 13.6cm)
Coaster: 4⅝ inches W x 4⅝ inches H (11.8cm x 11.8cm)

Skill Level: Beginner

Materials

- ❑ 7-count plastic canvas:
  - 3 sheets clear
  - 1½ sheets white
- ❑ Worsted weight yarn as listed in color key
- ❑ Metallic craft cord as listed in color key
- ❑ #16 tapestry needle
- ❑ Hot-glue gun *or* clear-drying craft glue

Stitching Step by Step

Coaster Holder

1 Cut front, back, right and left sides, bottom, two supports, two roofs, one awning top and two awning sides from clear plastic canvas according to graphs.

2 Stitch plastic canvas according to graphs, reversing one awning side before stitching, and filling in uncoded areas on roofs, front, back and right side with dark yellow Continental Stitches. Supports and bottom will remain unstitched. Leave red line on front unstitched; it will be used for attaching awning later.

3 Using white yarn throughout, Whipstitch supports to left side and coaster holder bottom as described in directions for Assembly in the General Instructions, above. Overcast remaining edges of supports and top edge of opening in left side.

4 Using dark yellow yarn through step 6, Whipstitch a straight edge of one awning side to one end of the awning top, with the diagonal edge of the awning side angling down and toward the back. In the same manner, Whipstitch the remaining awning side to the other end of the awning top.

5 Overcast remaining edges of awning sides and front (scalloped) edge of awning top.

6 Whipstitch back (straight) edge of awning top to coaster holder front where indicated by red line on graph.

7 Using white yarn throughout, Whipstitch front, left side, back and right side together along corners. Whipstitch assembled walls to unstitched bottom, Overcasting bottom edge of opening in left side. Overcast all top edges. Tack supports to right and left sides to hold them securely.

8 Using yellow yarn, Whipstitch roof pieces together along one long edge. Overcast remaining edges.

9 Glue roof to pet shop; glue back (diagonal) edges of awning sides to front of pet shop.

Coasters

1 Cut six coasters from clear plastic canvas and six coasters from white plastic canvas according to graph.

2 Stitch clear plastic canvas coasters according to graph, filling in uncoded areas with white Continental Stitches. White coasters will be used for backing and will remain unstitched.

3 When background stitching is complete, Backstitch puppies' mouths using 2 plies separated from a length of black yarn.

4 Using white yarn, Whipstitch a white coaster to the wrong side of each stitched coaster.

5 Insert coasters in coaster holder through slot in left side.

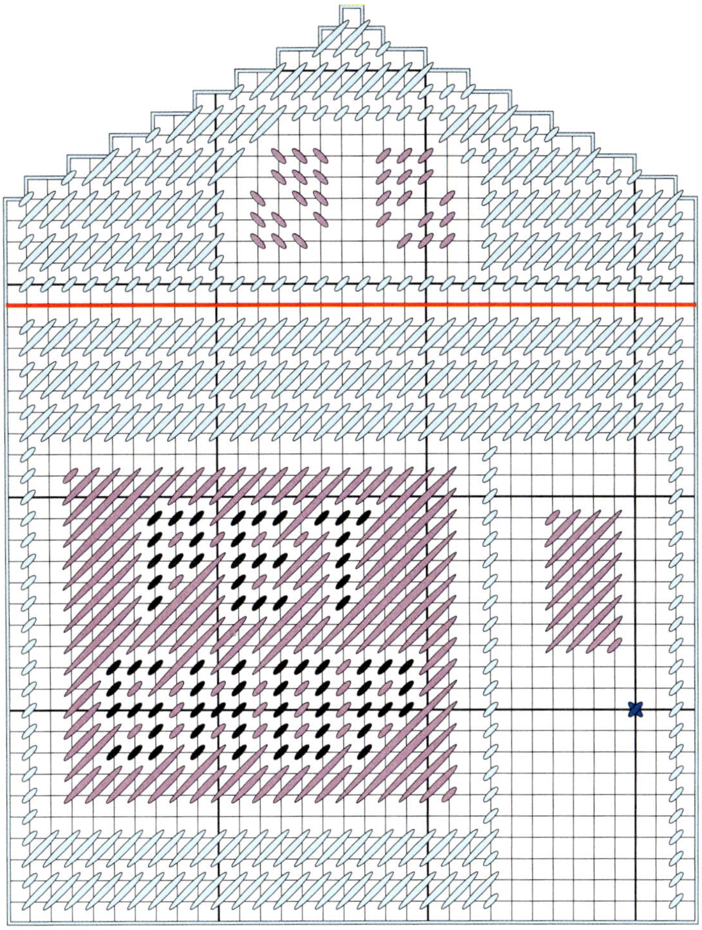

Pet Shop Front
33 holes x 43 holes
Cut 1 from clear plastic canvas

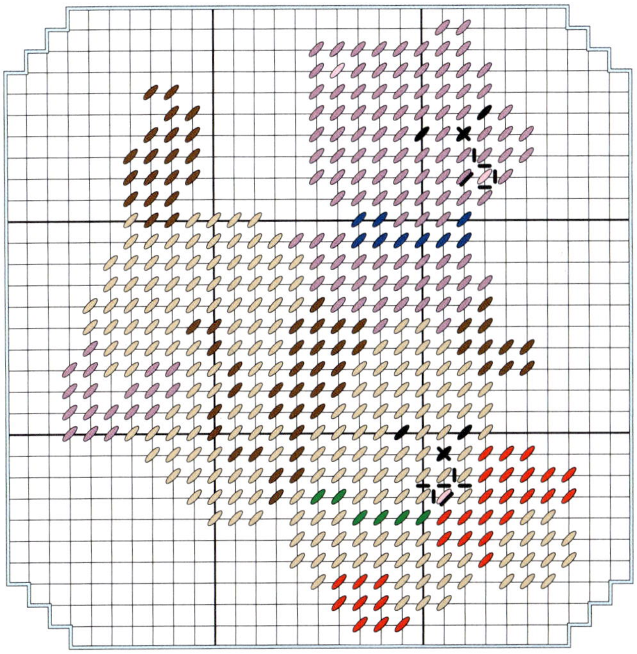

Pet Shop Coaster
30 holes x 30 holes
Cut 6 from clear plastic canvas;
stitch as shown
Cut 6 from white plastic canvas;
leave unstitched

COLOR KEY

Yards	Worsted Weight Yarn
70 (64m)	White
19 (17.4m)	Light gray
15 (13.7m)	Beige
12 (11m)	Yellow
6 (5.5m)	Light brown
3 (2.7m)	Black
3 (2.7m)	Off-white
1 (0.9m)	Pink
22 (20.1m)	Uncoded areas on coaster holder are dark yellow Continental Stitches
	Uncoded areas on coasters are white Continental Stitches
	Dark yellow Straight Stitch
	Yellow Straight Stitch
	White Straight Stitch
	Black 2-ply Backstitch
	Metallic Craft Cord
1 (0.9m)	Silver
1 (0.9m)	Gold

Pet Shop Back
33 holes x 43 holes
Cut 1 from clear plastic canvas

Pet Shop Right Side
24 holes x 34 holes
Cut 1 from clear plastic canvas

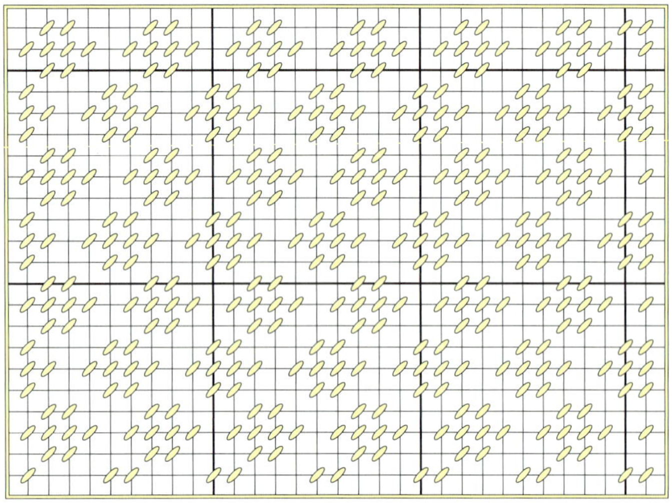

Pet Shop Roof
32 holes x 23 holes
Cut 2 from clear plastic canvas

COLOR KEY

Yards	Worsted Weight Yarn
70 (64m)	White
19 (17.4m)	Light gray
15 (13.7m)	Beige
12 (11m)	Yellow
6 (5.5m)	Light brown
3 (2.7m)	Black
3 (2.7m)	Off-white
1 (0.9m)	Pink
22 (20.1m)	Uncoded areas on coaster holder are dark yellow Continental Stitches
	Uncoded areas on coasters are white Continental Stitches
	Dark yellow Straight Stitch
	Yellow Straight Stitch
	White Straight Stitch
	Black 2-ply Backstitch
	Metallic Craft Cord
1 (0.9m)	Silver
1 (0.9m)	Gold

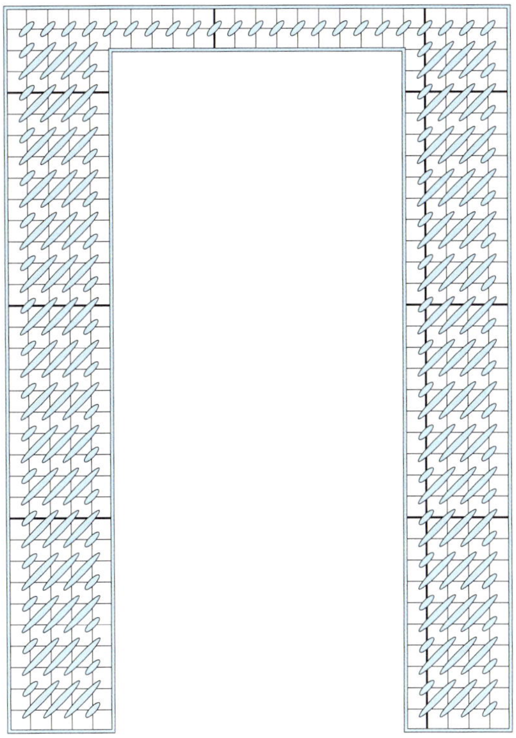

Pet Shop Left Side
24 holes x 34 holes
Cut 1 from clear plastic canvas

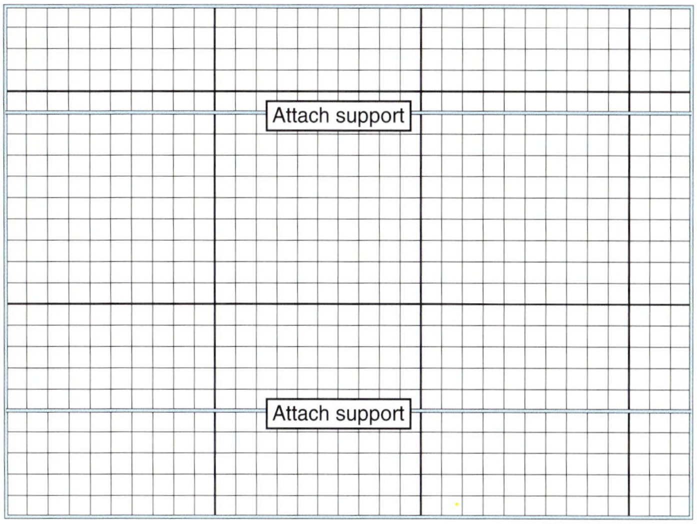

Pet Shop Bottom
33 holes x 24 holes
Cut 1 from clear plastic canvas;
leave unstitched

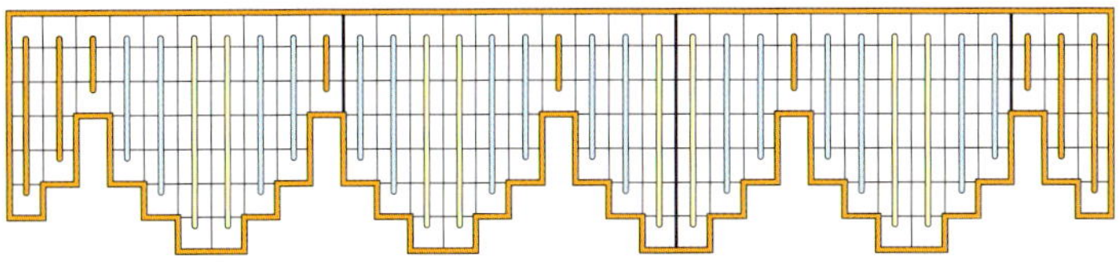

Pet Shop Awning Top
33 holes x 7 holes
Cut 1 from clear plastic canvas

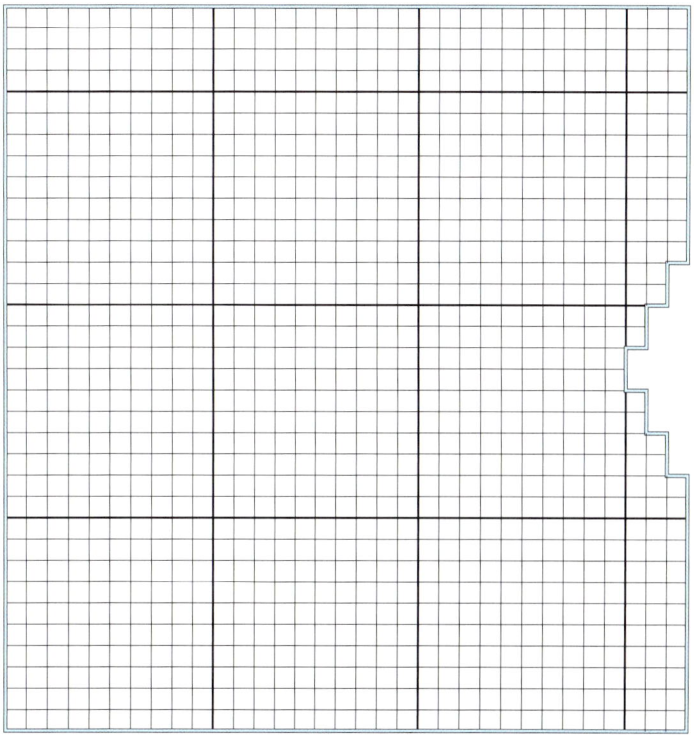

Pet Shop Support
33 holes x 34 holes
Cut 2 from clear plastic canvas;
leave unstitched

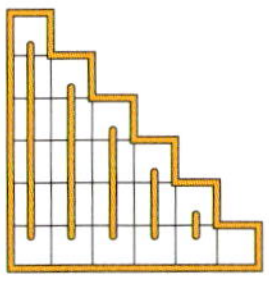

Pet Shop Awning Side
6 holes x 6 holes
Cut 2 from clear plastic canvas;
reverse 1 before stitching

Barn

Size: **Coaster Holder:** 6⅛ inches W x 7¼ inches H x 4¾ inches D (15.6cm x 18.4cm x 12.1cm)
Coaster: 4⅝ inches W x 4⅝ inches H (11.8cm x 11.8cm)
Skill Level: Beginner

Materials

- ❑ 7-count plastic canvas:
  - 3 sheets clear
  - 1½ sheets light blue
- ❑ Worsted weight yarn as listed in color key
- ❑ Metallic craft cord as listed in color key
- ❑ #16 tapestry needle
- ❑ Hot-glue gun *or* clear-drying craft glue

Stitching Step by Step

Coaster Holder

1 Cut front, back, right and left sides, bottom, two supports and two roofs from clear plastic canvas according to graphs.

2 Stitch plastic canvas according to graphs, filling in uncoded areas on front and back with red Continental Stitches. Supports and bottom will remain unstitched.

3 Using red yarn through step 4, Whipstitch supports to left side and coaster holder bottom as described in directions for Assembly in the General Instructions, page 1. Overcast remaining edges of supports and top edge of opening in left side.

4 Whipstitch front, left side, back and right side together along corners. Whipstitch assembled walls to unstitched bottom, Overcasting bottom edge of opening in left side. Overcast all top edges. Tack supports to right and left sides to hold them securely.

5 Using light brown yarn, Whipstitch roof pieces together along one long edge. Overcast remaining edges.

6 Glue roof to barn.

Coasters

1 Cut six coasters from clear plastic canvas and six coasters from light blue plastic canvas according to graph.

2 Stitch clear plastic canvas coasters according to graph, filling in uncoded areas with light blue Continental Stitches. Light blue coasters will be used for backing and will remain unstitched.

3 Using light blue yarn, Whipstitch a light blue coaster to the wrong side of each stitched coaster.

4 Insert coasters in coaster holder through slot in left side.

COLOR KEY

Yards	Worsted Weight Yarn
39 (35.7m)	Red
23 (21m)	Light brown
13 (11.9m)	White
3 (2.7m)	Black
3 (2.7m)	Medium brown
2 (1.8m)	Peach
2 (1.8m)	Very light gold
1 (0.9m)	Off-white
42 (38.4m)	Uncoded areas on coaster are light blue Continental Stitches
	Uncoded areas on coaster holder are red Continental Stitches
	Light blue Whipstitch
	Metallic Craft Cord
1 (0.9m)	Gold

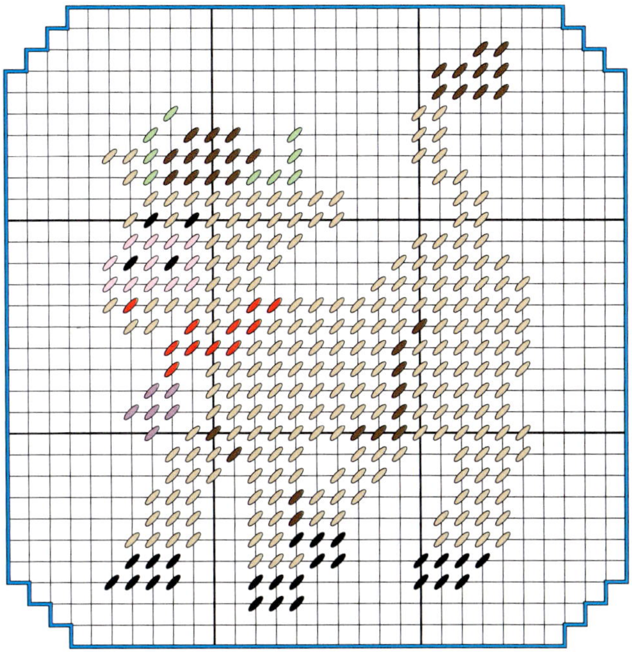

Barn Coaster
30 holes x 30 holes
Cut 6 from clear plastic canvas; stitch as shown
Cut 6 from light blue plastic canvas; leave unstitched

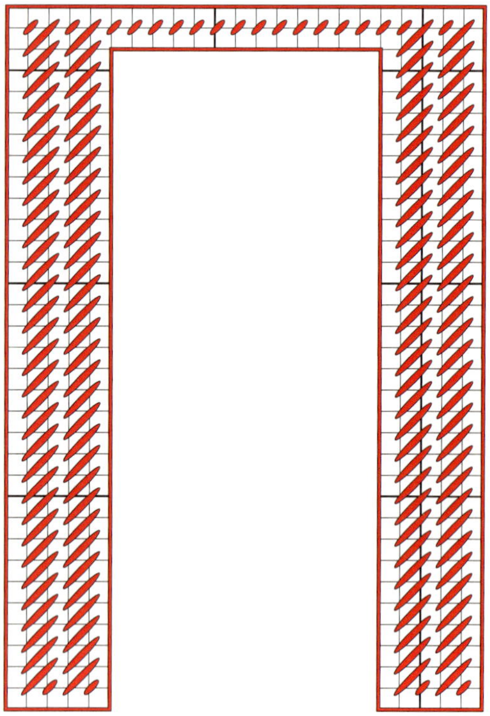

Barn Left Side
23 holes x 33 holes
Cut 1 from clear plastic canvas

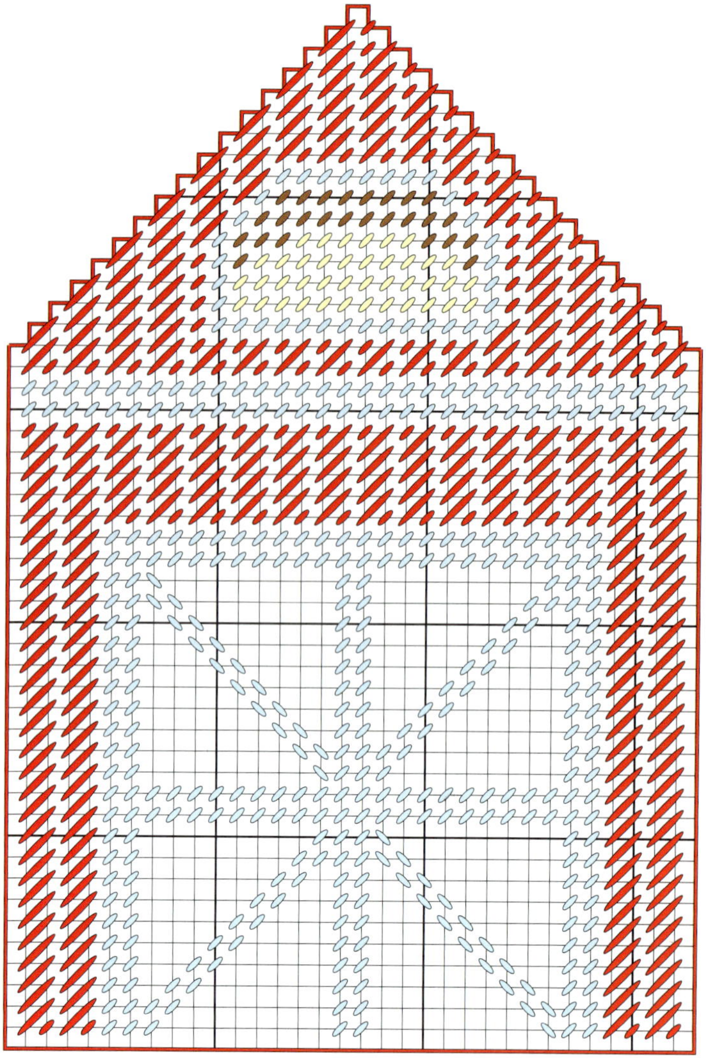

Barn Front
33 holes x 49 holes
Cut 1 from clear plastic canvas

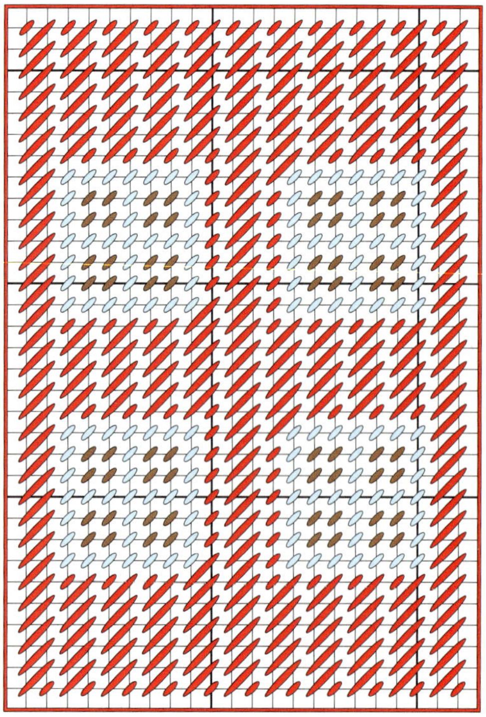

Barn Right Side
23 holes x 33 holes
Cut 1 from clear plastic canvas

COLOR KEY

Yards	Worsted Weight Yarn
39 (35.7m)	Red
23 (21m)	Light brown
13 (11.9m)	White
3 (2.7m)	Black
3 (2.7m)	Medium brown
2 (1.8m)	Peach
2 (1.8m)	Very light gold
1 (0.9m)	Off-white
42 (38.4m)	Uncoded areas on coaster are light blue Continental Stitches
	Uncoded areas on coaster holder are red Continental Stitches
	Light blue Whipstitch
	Metallic Craft Cord
1 (0.9m)	Gold

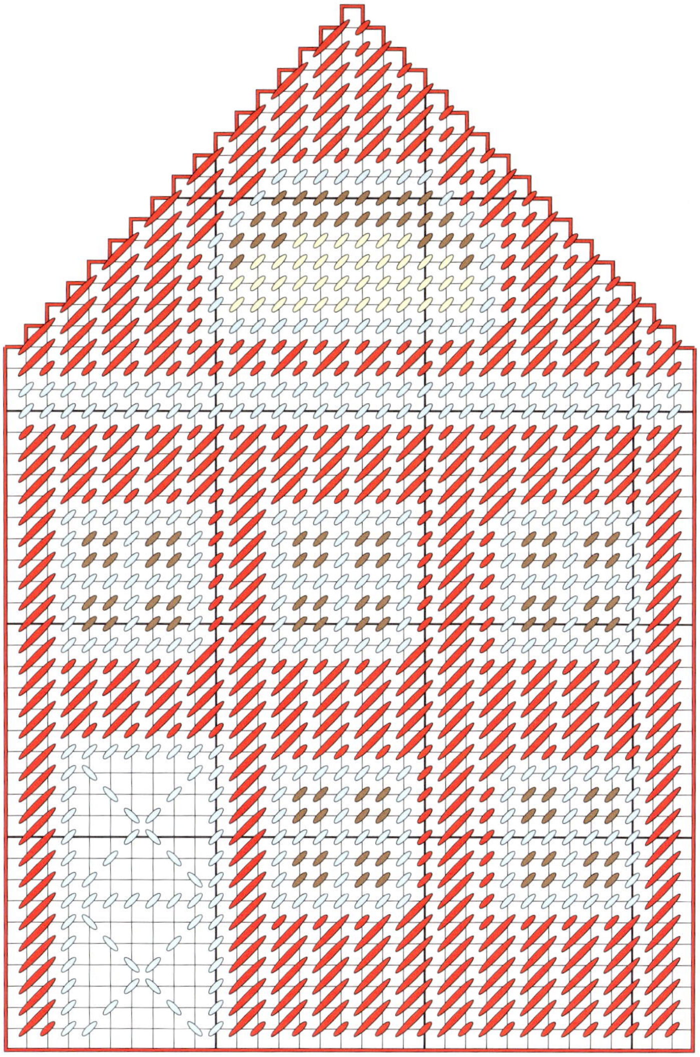

Barn Back
33 holes x 49 holes
Cut 1 from clear plastic canvas

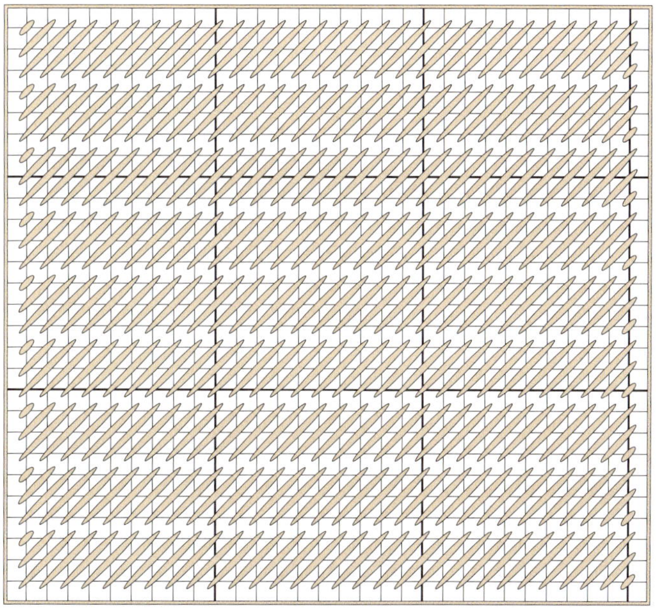

Barn Roof
31 holes x 28 holes
Cut 2 from clear plastic canvas

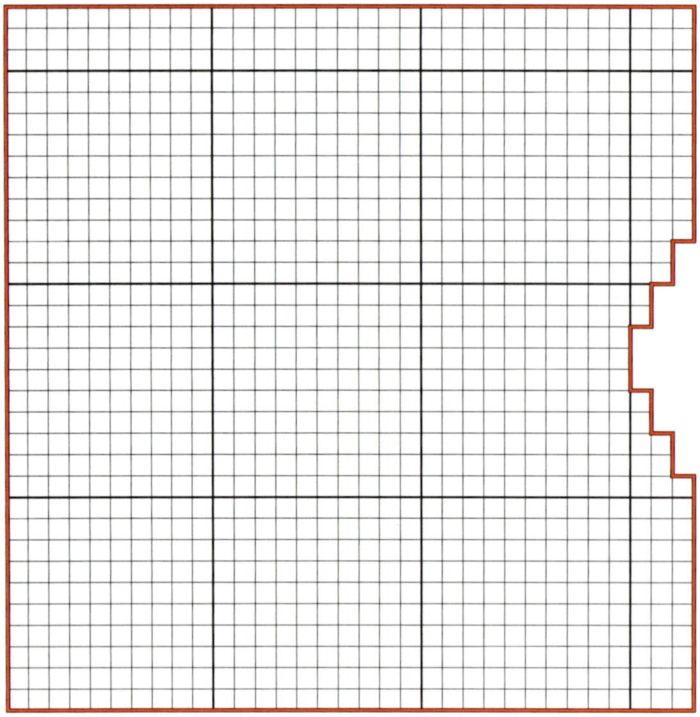

Barn Support
33 holes x 33 holes
Cut 2 from clear plastic canvas;
leave unstitched

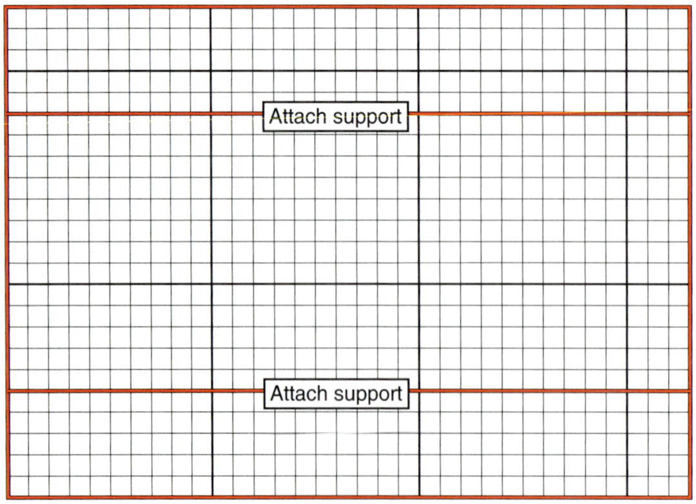

Barn Bottom
33 holes x 23 holes
Cut 1 from clear plastic canvas;
leave unstitched

Fire Department

Size: **Coaster Holder:** 5 inches W x 6⅜ inches H x 3¾ inches D (12.7cm x 16.2cm x 9.5cm)
Coaster: 4½ inches W x 4½ inches H (11.4cm x 11.4cm)

Skill Level: Beginner

Materials

- ❑ 4 sheets clear 7-count plastic canvas
- ❑ Worsted weight yarn as listed in color key
- ❑ #16 tapestry needle

Stitching Step by Step

Coaster Holder

1 Cut front, back, right and left sides, bottom, two supports and roof from clear plastic canvas according to graphs.

2 Stitch plastic canvas according to graphs, filling in uncoded areas with off-white Continental Stitches. Supports and bottom will remain unstitched.

3 Using red yarn through step 4, Whipstitch supports to left side and coaster holder bottom as described in directions for Assembly in the General Instructions, page 1. Overcast remaining edges of supports and top edge of opening in left side.

4 Whipstitch front, left side, back and right side together along corners. Whipstitch assembled walls to unstitched bottom, Overcasting bottom edge of opening in left side. Overcast top edge of front between arrows. Tack supports to right and left sides to hold them securely.

5 Using dark gray yarn, Overcast front edge of roof between arrows. Using red yarn, Whipstitch roof to fire department along remaining edges.

Coasters

1 Cut 12 coasters from clear plastic canvas according to graph.

2 Stitch six plastic canvas coasters according to graph, filling in uncoded areas with off-white Continental Stitches. Remaining coasters will be used for backing and will remain unstitched.

3 When background stitching is complete, Backstitch bear's mouth, emblem on fire hat and nozzle on fire hose using 2 plies separated from a length of black yarn.

4 Using off-white yarn, Whipstitch an unstitched coaster to the wrong side of each stitched coaster.

5 Insert coasters in coaster holder through slot in left side.

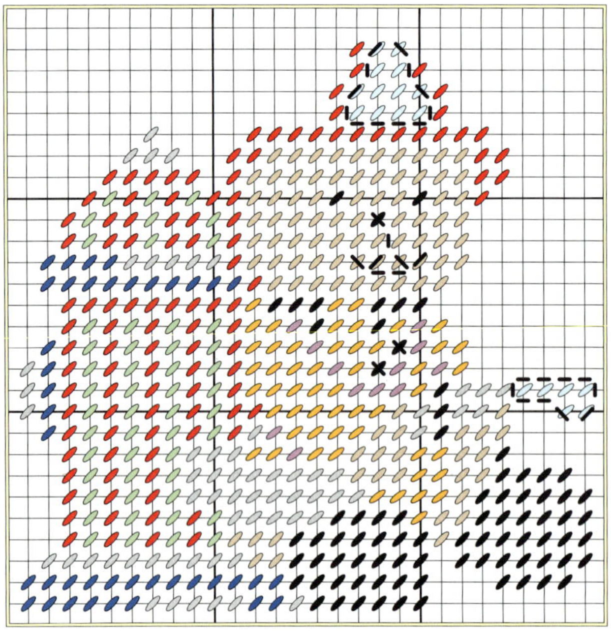

Fire Department Coaster
29 holes x 29 holes
Cut 12 from clear plastic canvas
Stitch 6 as shown; leave 6 unstitched

COLOR KEY

Yards	Worsted Weight Yarn
35 (32m)	Red
16 (14.6m)	Dark gray
11 (10.1m)	Black
8 (7.3m)	Medium brown
6 (5.5m)	Gray
5 (4.6m)	Dark red
5 (4.6m)	Yellow
3 (2.7m)	Very dark gray
2 (1.8m)	Dark yellow
2 (1.8m)	White
42 (38.4m)	Uncoded areas on coasters and coaster holder are off-white Continental Stitches
	Off-white Whipstitch
	Black 2-ply Backstitch

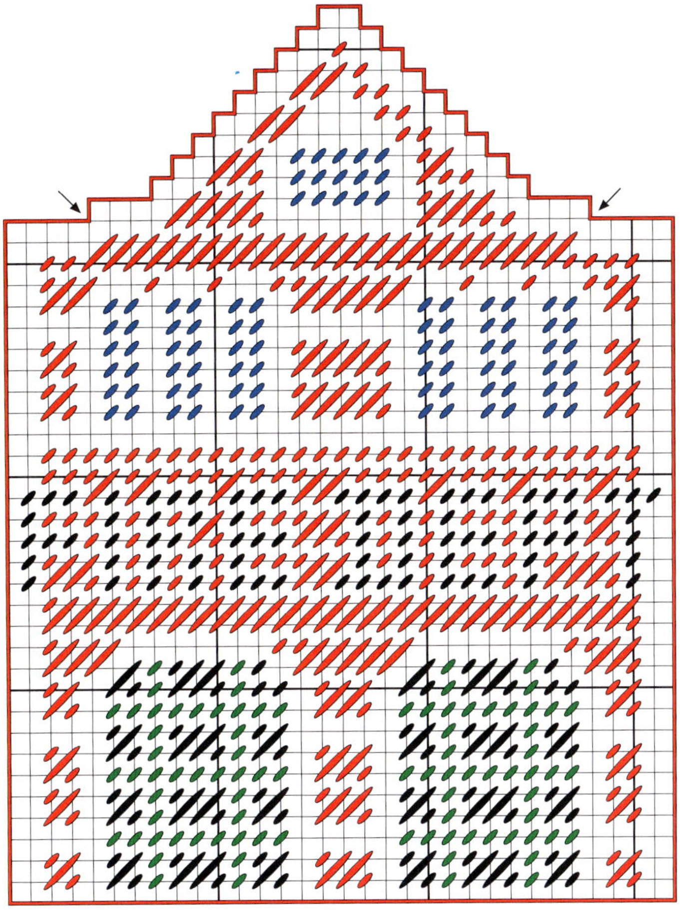

Fire Department Front
32 holes x 42 holes
Cut 1 from clear plastic canvas

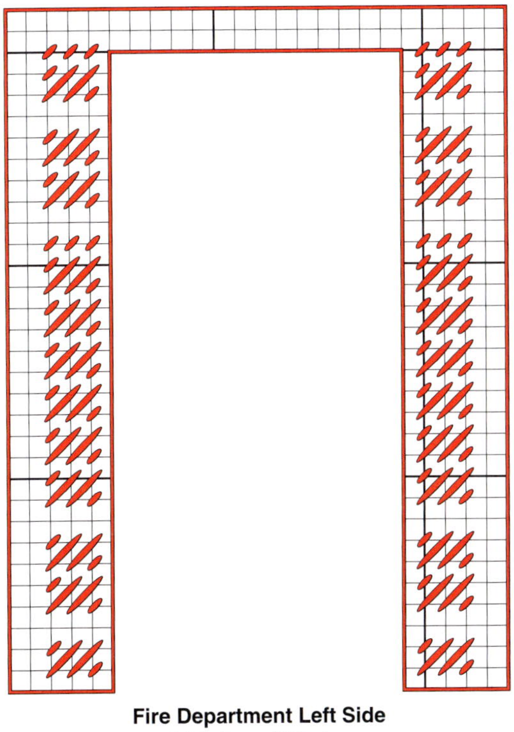

Fire Department Left Side
24 holes x 32 holes
Cut 1 from clear plastic canvas

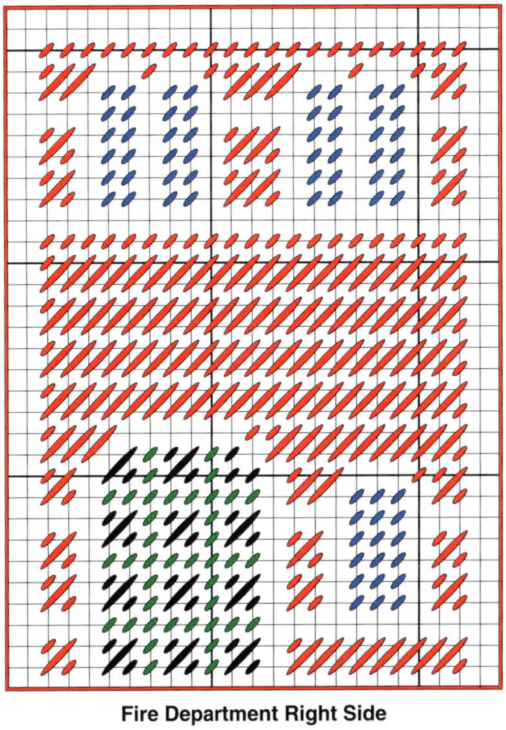

Fire Department Right Side
24 holes x 32 holes
Cut 1 from clear plastic canvas

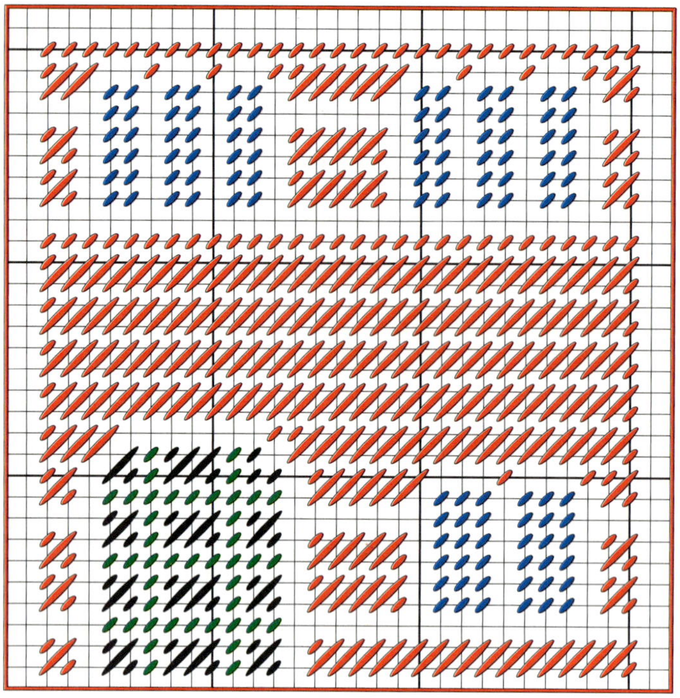

Fire Department Back
32 holes x 32 holes
Cut 1 from clear plastic canvas

COLOR KEY	
Yards	**Worsted Weight Yarn**
35 (32m)	Red
16 (14.6m)	Dark gray
11 (10.1m)	Black
8 (7.3m)	Medium brown
6 (5.5m)	Gray
5 (4.6m)	Dark red
5 (4.6m)	Yellow
3 (2.7m)	Very dark gray
2 (1.8m)	Dark yellow
2 (1.8m)	White
42 (38.4m)	Uncoded areas on coasters and coaster holder are off-white Continental Stitches
	Off-white Whipstitch
	Black 2-ply Backstitch

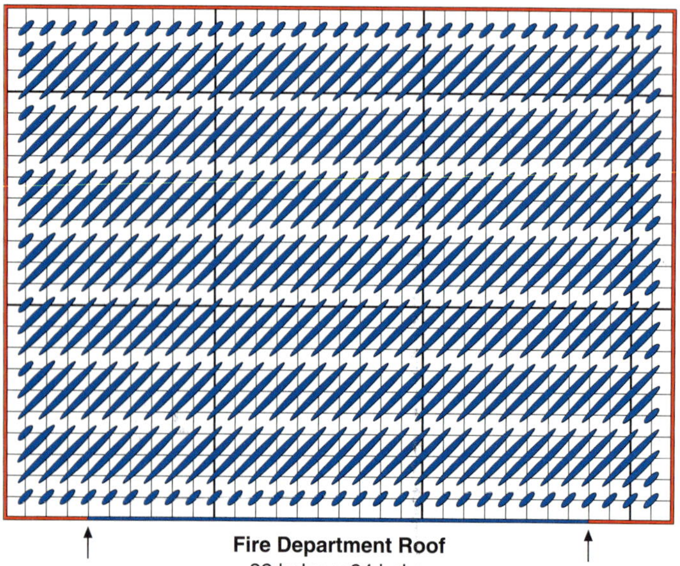

Fire Department Roof
32 holes x 24 holes
Cut 1 from clear plastic canvas

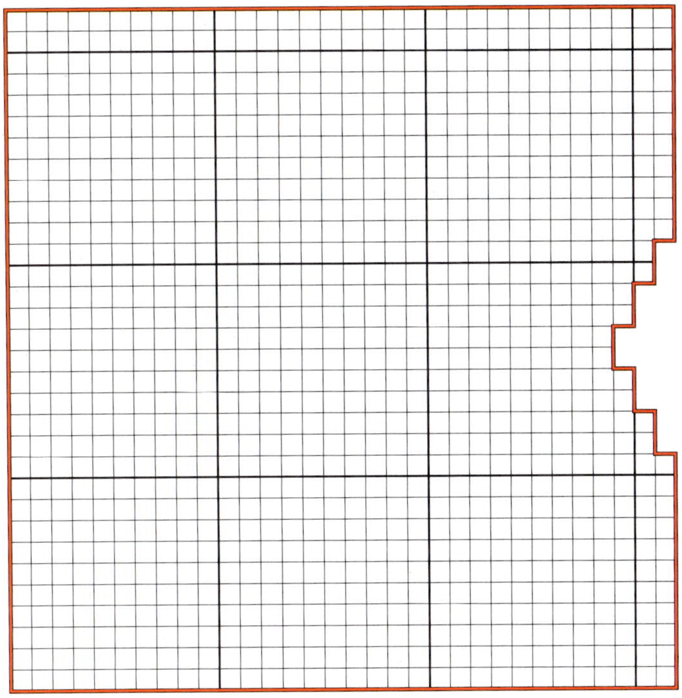

Fire Department Support
32 holes x 32 holes
Cut 2 from clear plastic canvas;
leave unstitched

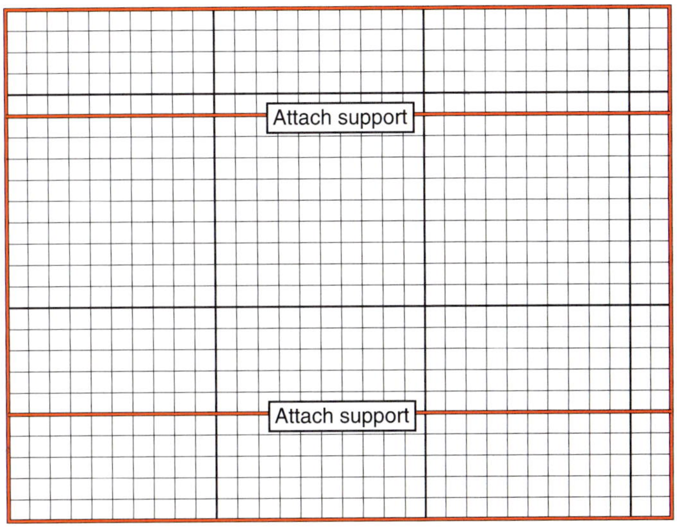

Fire Department Bottom
32 holes x 24 holes
Cut 1 from clear plastic canvas;
leave unstitched

Grocery Store

Size: **Coaster Holder:** 6 inches W x 7 inches H x 4¾ inches D (15.2cm x 17.8cm x 12.1cm)
Coaster: 4¾ inches W x 4¾ inches H (12.1cm x 12.1cm)

Skill Level: Beginner

Materials

- ❑ 7-count plastic canvas:
  - 3 sheets clear
  - 1½ sheets white
- ❑ Worsted weight yarn as listed in color key
- ❑ #16 tapestry needle
- ❑ Hot-glue gun *or* clear-drying craft glue

Stitching Step by Step

Coaster Holder

1 Cut front, back, right and left sides, bottom, two supports, two roofs, one dormer front, one dormer roof and two dormer sides from clear plastic canvas according to graphs.

2 Stitch plastic canvas according to graphs, filling in uncoded areas with off-white Continental Stitches. Supports and bottom will remain unstitched.

3 When background stitching is complete, Straight Stitch crosshatch pattern over windows on front and dormer front using 2 plies separated from a length of light brown yarn.

4 Using off-white and brick yarns according to graphs, Whipstitch supports to left side and coaster holder bottom as described in directions for Assembly in the General Instructions, page 1. Overcast remaining edges of supports and top edge of opening in left side.

5 Using brick yarn, Whipstitch front to left side and right side along corners. Using brick and white yarns throughout, Whipstitch back to left side and right side according to graphs; Whipstitch assembled walls to unstitched bottom, Overcasting bottom edge of opening in left side. Overcast all top edges. Tack supports to right and left sides to hold them securely.

6 Using medium brown yarn through step 9, Whipstitch roof pieces together along one long edge. Overcast remaining edges.

7 Overcast the back edge of the dormer roof and the bottom edge of the dormer front.

8 Whipstitch a straight edge of one dormer side to one end of the dormer front, with the diagonal edge of the dormer side angling down and toward the back. In the same manner, Whipstitch the remaining dormer side to the other end of the dormer front.

9 Whipstitch the ends of the dormer roof to the remaining straight edges of the dormer sides and front part of roof to top of front piece. Overcast the remaining edges of the dormer sides.

10 Referring to the photo throughout, glue the dormer to the front of the roof. Glue the roof to the grocery store.

Coasters

1 Cut six coasters from clear plastic canvas and six coasters from white plastic canvas according to graph.

2 Stitch clear plastic canvas coasters according to graph, filling in uncoded areas with off-white Continental Stitches. White coasters will be used for backing and will remain unstitched.

3 When background stitching is complete, Backstitch banana using 2 plies separated from a length of gold yarn; Backstitch grapes using 2 plies separated from a length of black yarn.

4 Using off-white yarn, Whipstitch a white coaster to the wrong side of each stitched coaster.

5 Insert coasters in coaster holder through slot in left side.

COLOR KEY

Yards	Worsted Weight Yarn
64 (58.5m)	Off-white
32 (29.3m)	Medium brown
13 (11.9m)	Brick
13 (11.9m)	Red
12 (11m)	Light brown
9 (8.2m)	Purple
6 (5.5m)	Gray
6 (5.5m)	Yellow
3 (2.7m)	Light green
2 (1.8m)	Medium green
2 (1.8m)	Dark red
1 (0.9m)	Dark brown
1 (0.9m)	Dark yellow
	Uncoded areas on coasters and coaster holder are off-white Continental Stitches
	Light brown 2-ply Straight Stitch
7 (6.4m)	Black 2-ply Backstitch
2 (1.8m)	Gold 2-ply Backstitch

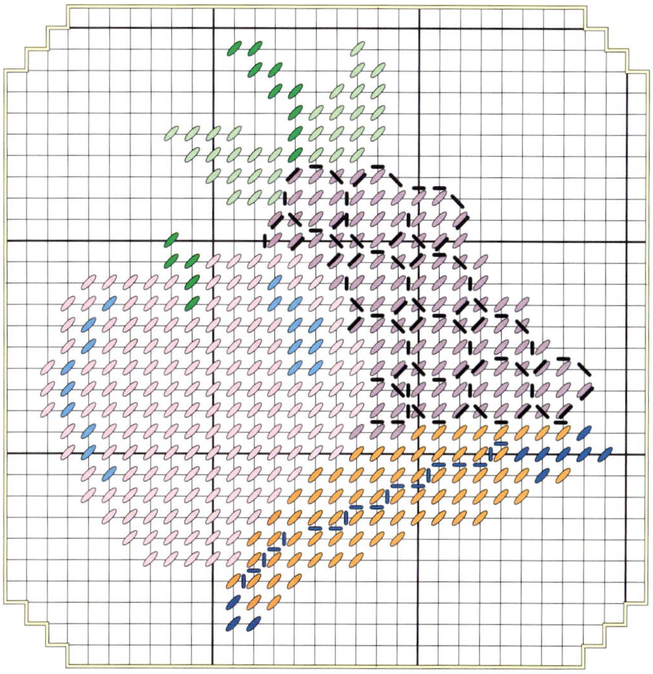

Grocery Store Coaster
31 holes x 31 holes
Cut 6 from clear plastic canvas; stitch as shown
Cut 6 from white plastic canvas; leave unstitched

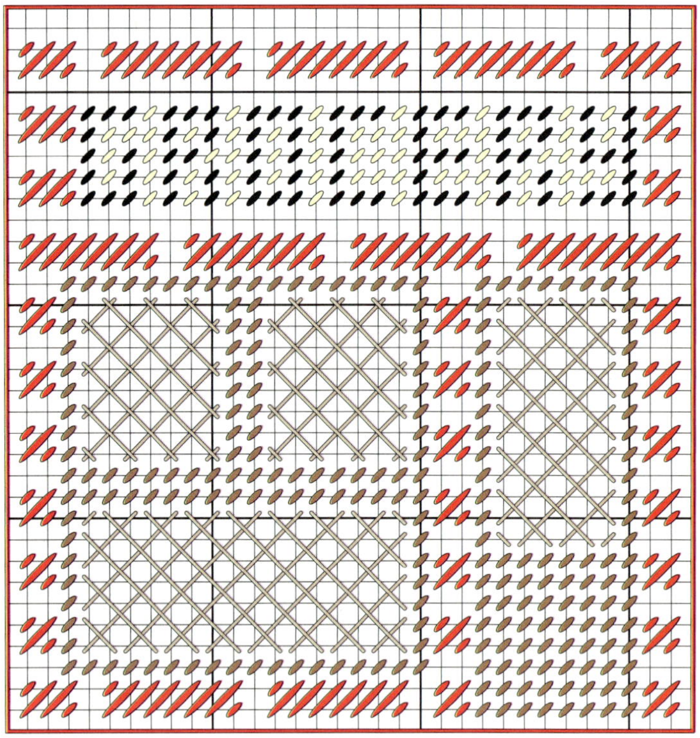

Grocery Store Front
33 holes x 34 holes
Cut 1 from clear plastic canvas

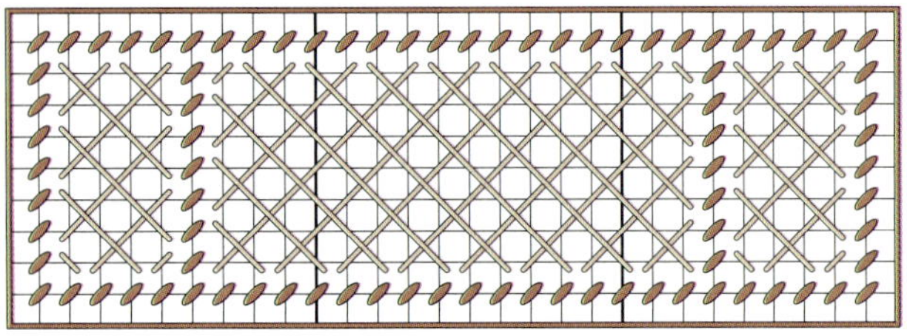

Grocery Store Dormer Front
29 holes x 10 holes
Cut 1 from clear plastic canvas

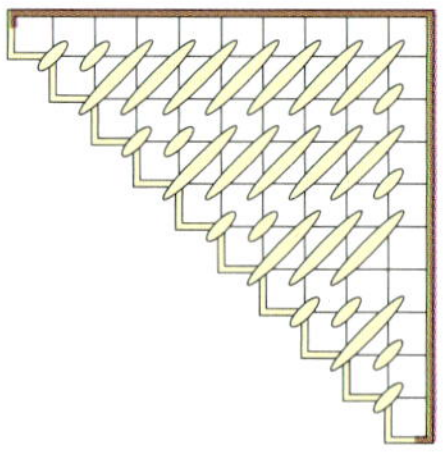

Grocery Store Dormer Side
10 holes x 10 holes
Cut 2 from clear plastic canvas;
reverse 1 before stitching

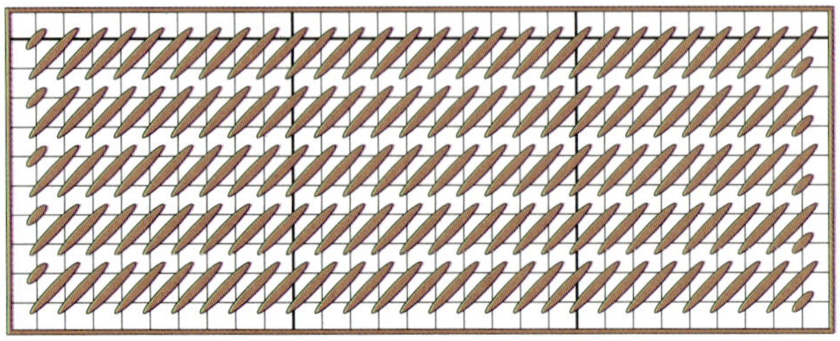

Grocery Store Dormer Roof
29 holes x 11 holes
Cut 1 from clear plastic canvas

COLOR KEY

Yards	Worsted Weight Yarn
64 (58.5m)	Off-white
32 (29.3m)	Medium brown
13 (11.9m)	Brick
13 (11.9m)	Red
12 (11m)	Light brown
9 (8.2m)	Purple
6 (5.5m)	Gray
6 (5.5m)	Yellow
3 (2.7m)	Light green
2 (1.8m)	Medium green
2 (1.8m)	Dark red
1 (0.9m)	Dark brown
1 (0.9m)	Dark yellow
	Uncoded areas on coasters and coaster holder are off-white Continental Stitches
	Light brown 2-ply Straight Stitch
7 (6.4m)	Black 2-ply Backstitch
2 (1.8m)	Gold 2-ply Backstitch

Grocery Store Right Side
24 holes x 45 holes
Cut 1 from clear plastic canvas

Grocery Store Back
33 holes x 34 holes
Cut 1 from clear plastic canvas

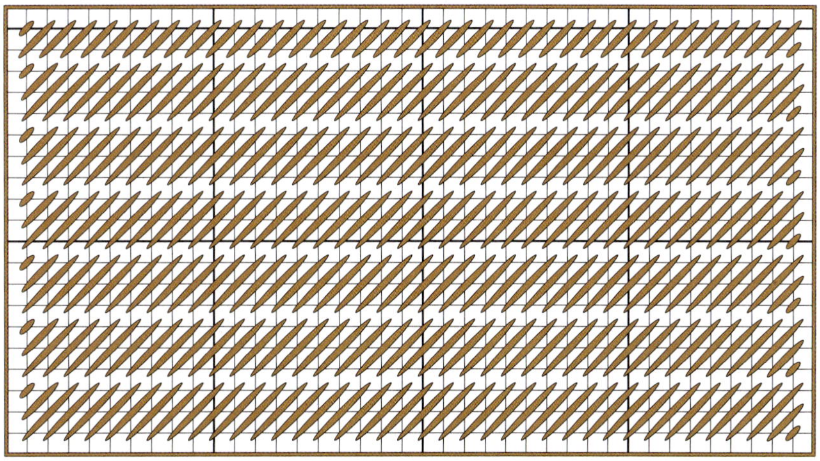

Grocery Store Roof
39 holes x 21 holes
Cut 2 from clear plastic canvas

Grocery Store Left Side
24 holes x 45 holes
Cut 1 from clear plastic canvas

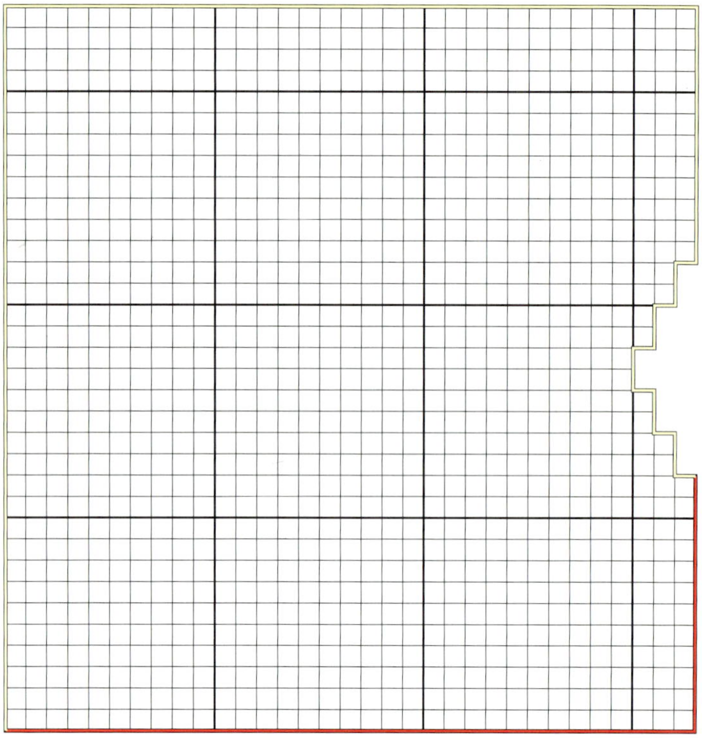

Grocery Support
33 holes x 34 holes
Cut 2 from clear plastic canvas;
leave unstitched

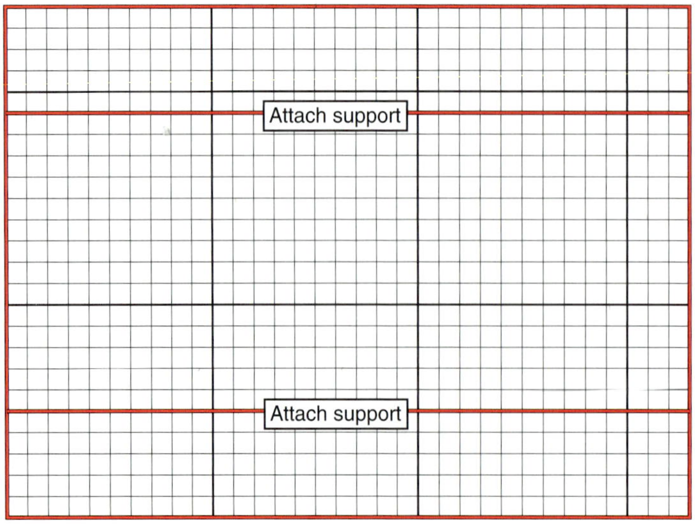

Grocery Store Bottom
33 holes x 24 holes
Cut 1 from clear plastic canvas;
leave unstitched

Schoolhouse

Size: **Coaster Holder:** 6⅛ inches W x 10¼ inches H x 4¾ inches D (15.6cm x 26cm x 12.1cm)
Coaster: 4½ inches W x 4½ inches H (11.4cm x 11.4cm)

Skill Level: Beginner

Materials

- ❑ 7-count plastic canvas:
  - 3 sheets clear
  - 1½ sheets light blue
- ❑ Worsted weight yarn as listed in color key
- ❑ #16 tapestry needle
- ❑ Small gold bell
- ❑ Hot-glue gun *or* clear-drying craft glue

Stitching Step by Step

Coaster Holder

1 Cut front, back, right and left sides, bottom, two supports, two roofs, two bell tower front/back pieces, two bell tower sides and four bell tower roofs from clear plastic canvas according to graphs.

2 Stitch plastic canvas according to graphs, filling in uncoded areas with white Continental Stitches. Supports and bottom will remain unstitched.

3 Using red yarn through step 4, Whipstitch supports to left side and coaster holder bottom as described in directions for Assembly in the General Instructions, page 1. Overcast remaining edges of supports and top edge of opening in left side.

4 Whipstitch front to left side and right side along corners. Whipstitch back to left side and right side according to graphs; Whipstitch assembled walls to unstitched bottom, Overcasting bottom edge of opening in left side. Overcast all top edges. Tack supports to right and left sides to hold them securely.

5 Using gray yarn, Whipstitch roof pieces together along one long edge. Overcast remaining edges.

6 Glue roof to schoolhouse.

7 Using white yarn throughout, Overcast openings in bell tower front, back and sides. Whipstitch bell tower front, back and sides together along corners; Overcast remaining edges. Referring to photo throughout, glue the bell tower to the schoolhouse roof.

8 Using gray yarn throughout, Whipstitch bell tower roof pieces together along long edges. Overcast remaining edges. Suspend bell from bell tower roof so that it will be visible through openings in bell tower. Glue roof with bell to bell tower.

Coasters

1 Cut six coasters from clear plastic canvas and six coasters from light blue plastic canvas according to graph.

2 Stitch clear plastic canvas coasters according to graph, filling in uncoded areas with light blue Continental Stitches. Light blue coasters will be used for backing and will remain unstitched.

3 Using light blue yarn, Whipstitch a light blue coaster to the wrong side of each stitched coaster.

4 Insert coasters in coaster holder through slot in left side.

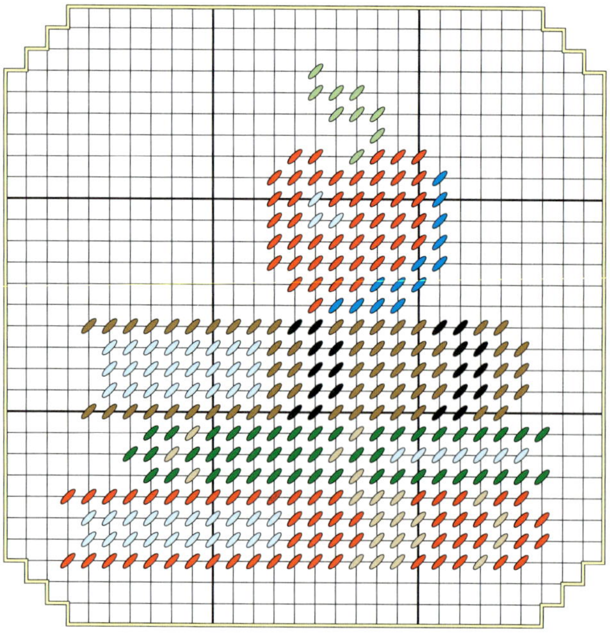

Schoolhouse Coaster
29 holes x 29 holes
Cut 6 from clear plastic canvas;
stitch as shown
Cut 6 from light blue plastic canvas;
leave unstitched

COLOR KEY	
Yards	**Worsted Weight Yarn**
44 (40.2m)	Red
28 (25.6m)	Gray
17 (15.5m)	White
5 (4.6m)	Yellow
5 (4.6m)	Light brown
4 (3.7m)	Royal blue
3 (2.7m)	Black
2 (1.8m)	Beige
1 (0.9m)	Medium green
1 (0.9m)	Dark red
43 (39.3m)	Uncoded areas on coasters are light blue Continental Stitches
	Uncoded areas on coaster holder are white Continental Stitches
	Light blue Whipstitch

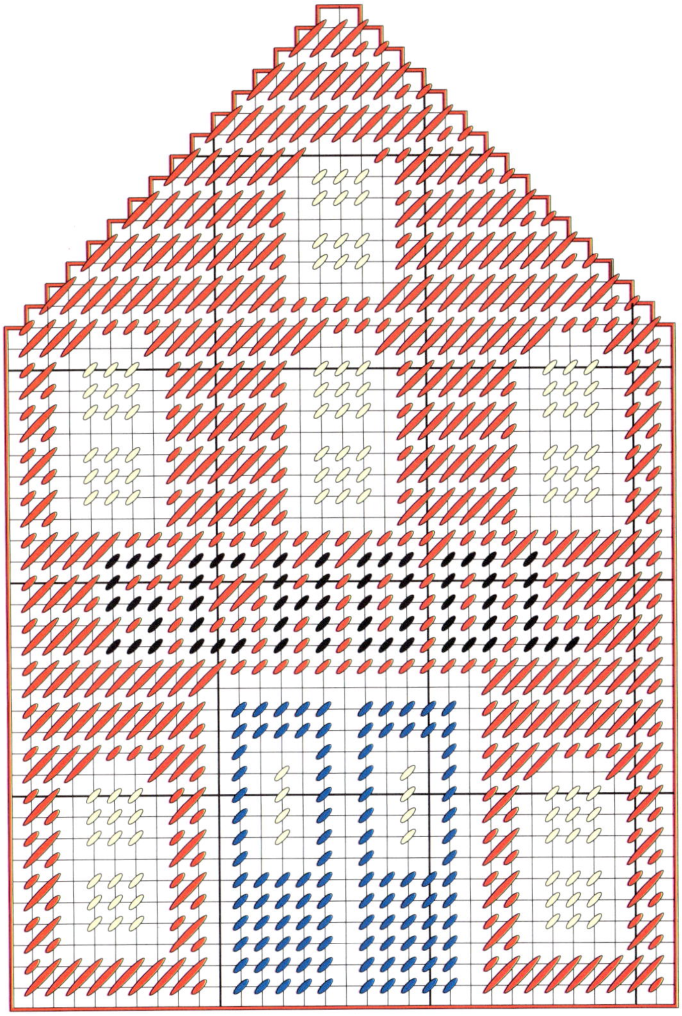

Schoolhouse Front
32 holes x 47 holes
Cut 1 from clear plastic canvas

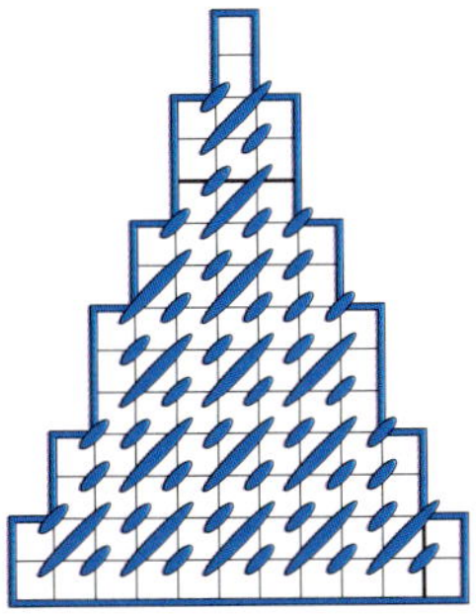

Bell Tower Roof
11 holes x 14 holes
Cut 4 from clear plastic canvas

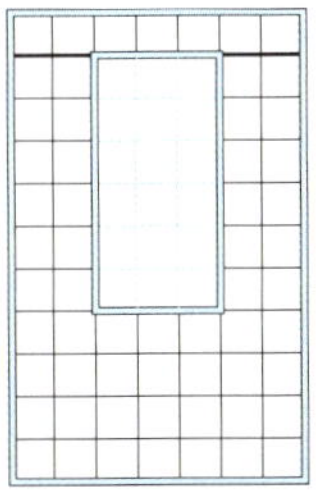

Bell Tower Side
7 holes x 11 holes
Cut 2 from clear plastic canvas,
cutting away center blue lines

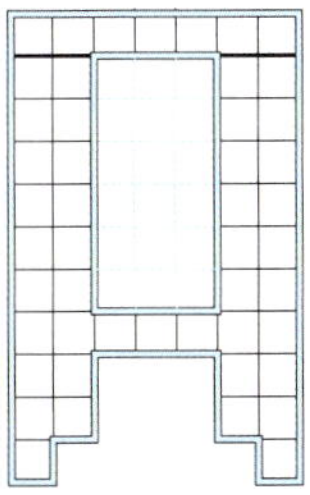

Bell Tower Front/Back
7 holes x 11 holes
Cut 2 from clear plastic canvas,
cutting away center blue lines

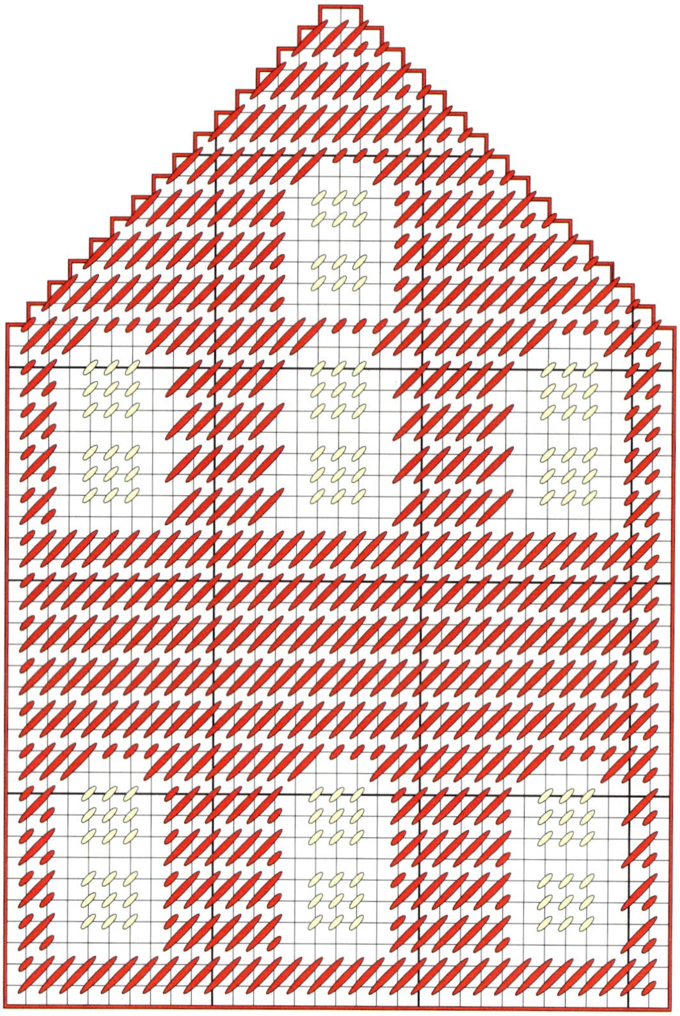

Schoolhouse Back
32 holes x 47 holes
Cut 1 from clear plastic canvas

COLOR KEY	
Yards	**Worsted Weight Yarn**
44 (40.2m)	Red
28 (25.6m)	Gray
17 (15.5m)	White
5 (4.6m)	Yellow
5 (4.6m)	Light brown
4 (3.7m)	Royal blue
3 (2.7m)	Black
2 (1.8m)	Beige
1 (0.9m)	Medium green
1 (0.9m)	Dark red
43 (39.3m)	Uncoded areas on coasters are light blue Continental Stitches
	Uncoded areas on coaster holder are white Continental Stitches
	Light blue Whipstitch

Schoolhouse Right Side
24 holes x 32 holes
Cut 1 from clear plastic canvas

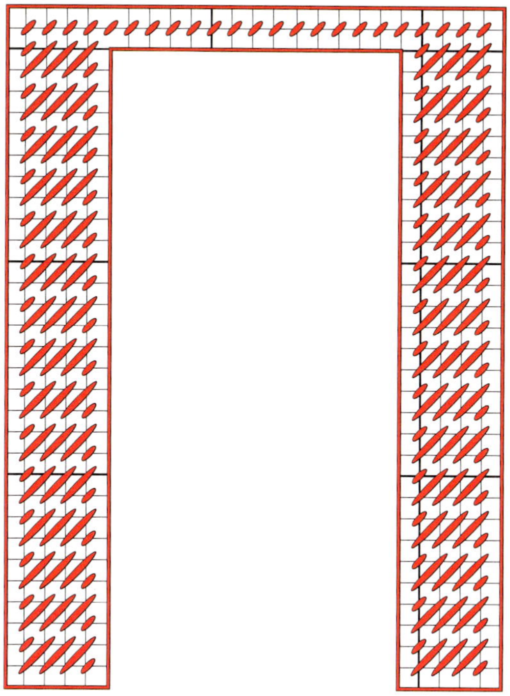

Schoolhouse Left Side
24 holes x 32 holes
Cut 1 from clear plastic canvas

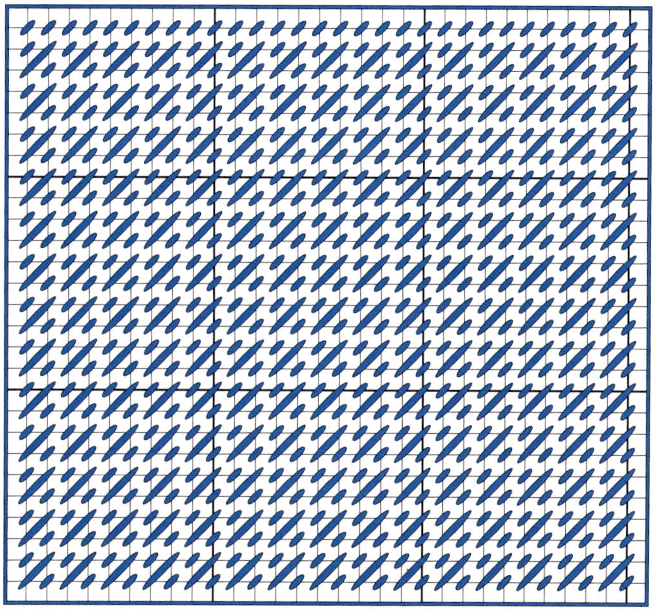

Schoolhouse Roof
31 holes x 28 holes
Cut 2 from clear plastic canvas

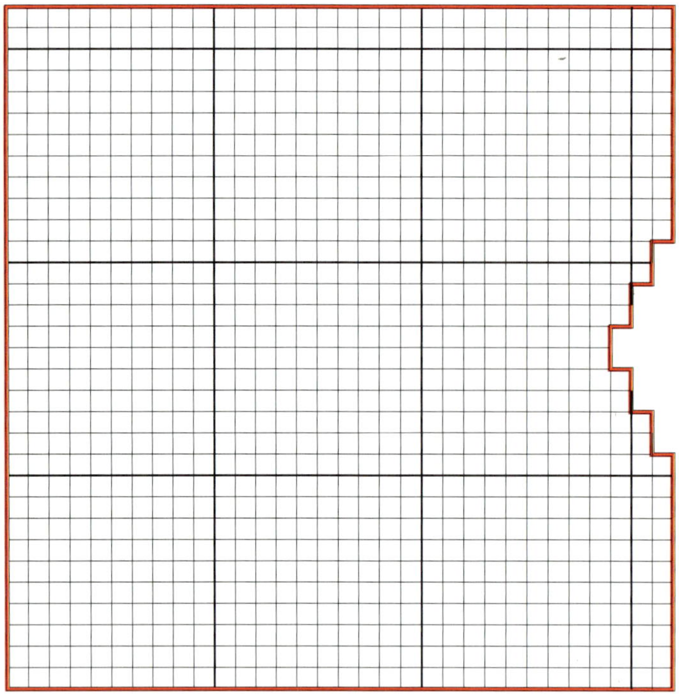

Schoolhouse Support
32 holes x 32 holes
Cut 2 from clear plastic canvas;
leave unstitched

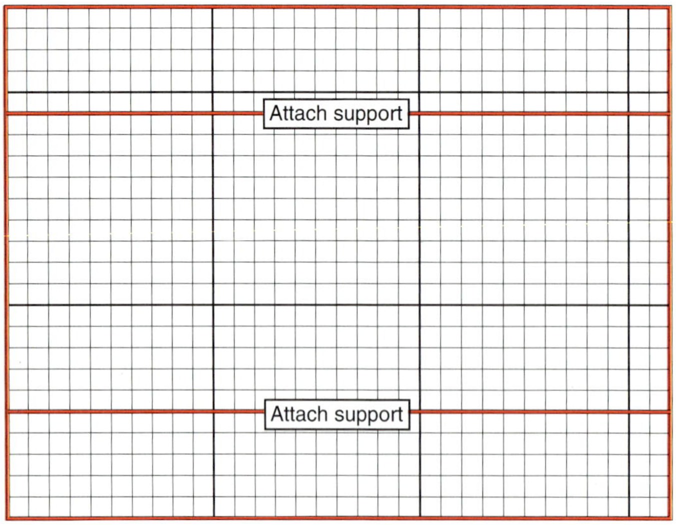

Schoolhouse Bottom
32 holes x 24 holes
Cut 1 from clear plastic canvas;
leave unstitched

Flower Shoppe

Size: **Coaster Holder:** 5⅞ inches W x 6¾ inches H x 4⅜ inches D (14.9cm x 17.2cm x 11.1cm)
Coaster: 4¾ inches W x 4¾ inches H (12.1cm x 12.1cm)

Skill Level: Beginner

Materials

- ❑ 7-count plastic canvas:
  - 3 sheets clear
  - 1½ sheets white
- ❑ Worsted weight yarn as listed in color key
- ❑ #16 tapestry needle
- ❑ Hot-glue gun *or* clear-drying craft glue

Stitching Step by Step

Coaster Holder

1 Cut front, back, right and left sides, bottom, two supports, roof front and back, two roof sides, rooftop, bay window front, two bay window sides and bay window roof from clear plastic canvas according to graphs.

2 Stitch plastic canvas according to graphs, leaving the unstitched area on the front according to graph. Fill in remaining uncoded areas with white Continental Stitches. Supports and bottom will remain unstitched. Leave red line on front unstitched; it will be used for attaching bay window later.

3 When background stitching is complete, Straight Stitch crosshatch pattern over windows on front, back, right side, bay front and bay sides using 2 plies separated from a length of white yarn.

4 Using light blue yarn, Whipstitch supports to left side and coaster holder bottom as described in directions for Assembly in the General Instructions, page 1. Overcast remaining edges of supports and top edge of opening in left side.

5 Using white yarn through step 7, Whipstitch bay window front between bay window sides along long edges. Overcast top and bottom edges.

6 Referring to photo throughout, Whipstitch edge of right-hand bay window side to flower shoppe front where indicated by vertical red Whipstitching line on graph.

7 Whipstitch left side of flower shoppe to edge of front and bay window's left-hand side panel, stitching through all three layers. Once bay window side has been attached, near top, switch to light blue yarn; continue Whipstitching walls together along corners.

8 Using light blue yarn throughout, Whipstitch remaining walls together along corners. Whipstitch assembled walls to unstitched bottom, Overcasting bottom edge of opening in left side; Overcast all top edges. Tack supports to right and left sides to hold them securely.

9 Using country blue yarn throughout, Whipstitch roof front, back and sides together along diagonal edges. Whipstitch rooftop to top edges. Overcast bottom edges. Glue roof to flower shoppe.

Coasters

1 Cut six coasters from clear plastic canvas and six coasters from white plastic canvas according to graph.

2 Stitch clear plastic canvas coasters according to graph, filling in uncoded areas with white Continental Stitches. White coasters will be used for backing and will remain unstitched.

3 Using white yarn, Whipstitch a white coaster to the wrong side of each stitched coaster.

4 Insert coasters in coaster holder through slot in left side.

COLOR KEY

Yards	Worsted Weight Yarn
43 (39.3m)	White
27 (24.7m)	Light blue
26 (23.8m)	Country blue
19 (17.4m)	Pink
16 (14.6m)	Rose
13 (11.9m)	Dark rose
10 (9.1m)	Dark olive
7 (6.4m)	Olive
4 (3.7m)	Yellow
4 (3.7m)	Light green
2 (1.8m)	Black
	Uncoded areas on coasters and coaster holder are white Continental Stiches
	White 2-ply Straight Stitch

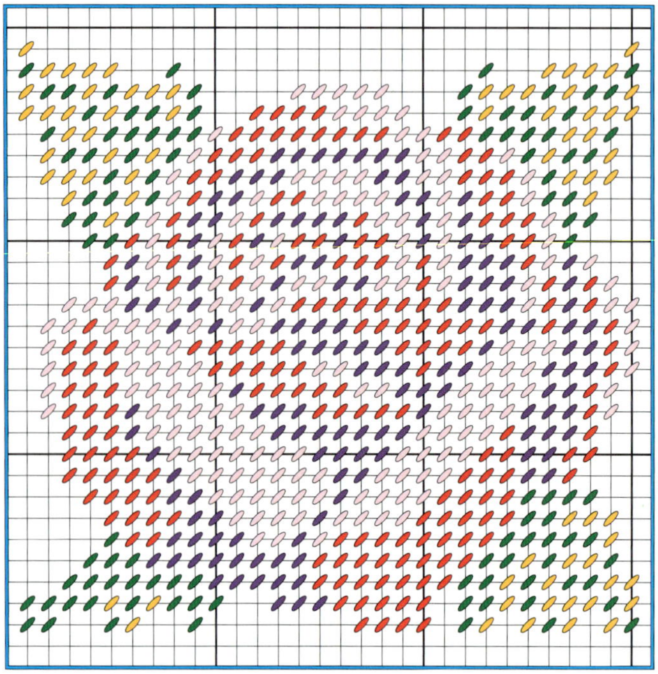

Flower Shoppe Coaster
31 holes x 31 holes
Cut 6 from clear plastic canvas;
stitch as shown
Cut 6 from white plastic canvas;
leave unstitched

Flower Shoppe Front
34 holes x 34 holes
Cut 1 from clear plastic canvas

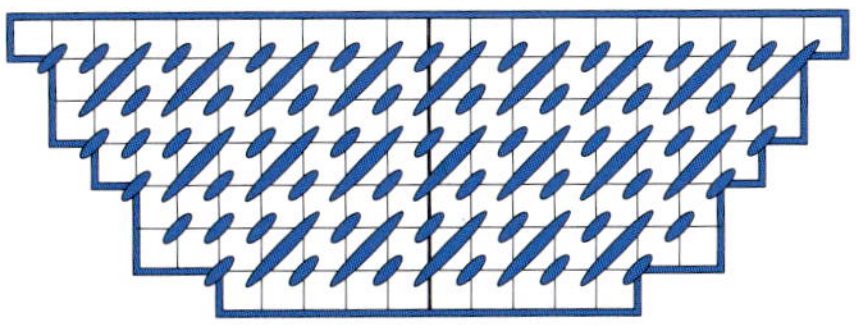

Flower Shoppe Bay Window Roof
20 holes x 7 holes
Cut 1 from clear plastic canvas

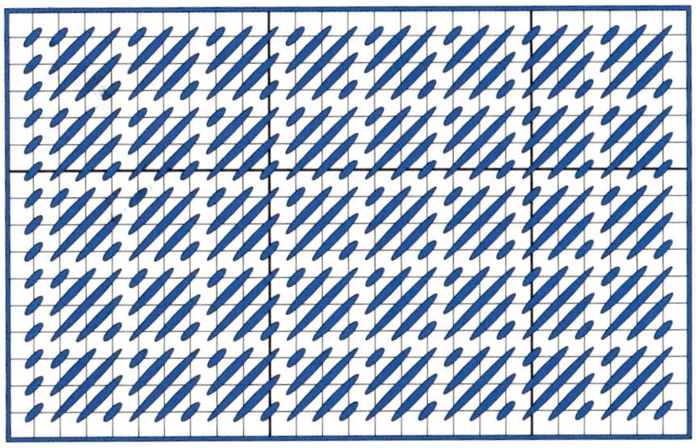

Flower Shoppe Rooftop
26 holes x 16 holes
Cut 1 from clear plastic canvas

Flower Shoppe Bay Window Side
6 holes x 30 holes
Cut 2 from clear plastic canvas

Flower Shoppe Back
34 holes x 34 holes
Cut 1 from clear plastic canvas

COLOR KEY	
Yards	**Worsted Weight Yarn**
43 (39.3m)	White
27 (24.7m)	Light blue
26 (23.8m)	Country blue
19 (17.4m)	Pink
16 (14.6m)	Rose
13 (11.9m)	Dark rose
10 (9.1m)	Dark olive
7 (6.4m)	Olive
4 (3.7m)	Yellow
4 (3.7m)	Light green
2 (1.8m)	Black
	Uncoded areas on coasters and coaster holder are white Continental Sitiches
	White 2-ply Straight Stitch

Flower Shoppe Right Side
24 holes x 34 holes
Cut 1 from clear plastic canvas

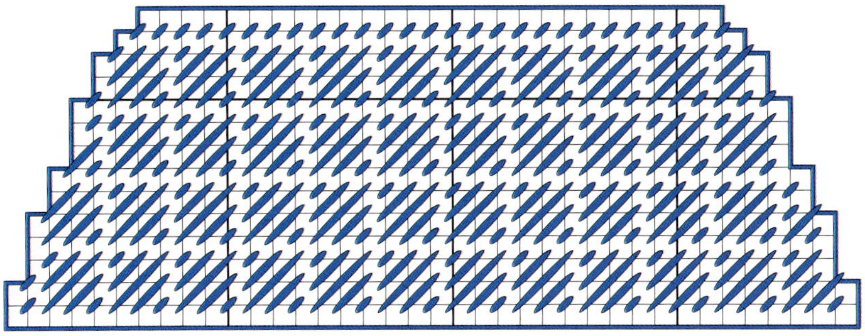

Flower Shoppe Roof Back
38 holes x 14 holes
Cut 1 from clear plastic canvas

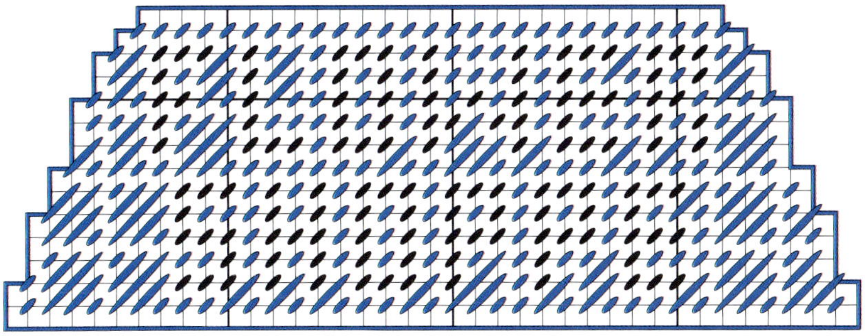

Flower Shoppe Roof Front
38 holes x 14 holes
Cut 1 from clear plastic canvas

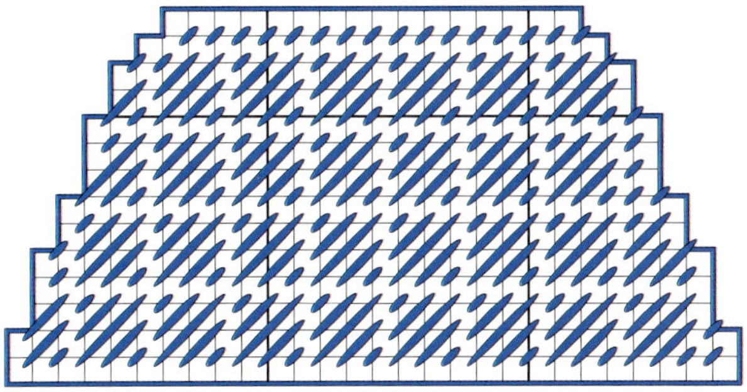

Flower Shoppe Roof Side
28 holes x 14 holes
Cut 2 from clear plastic canvas

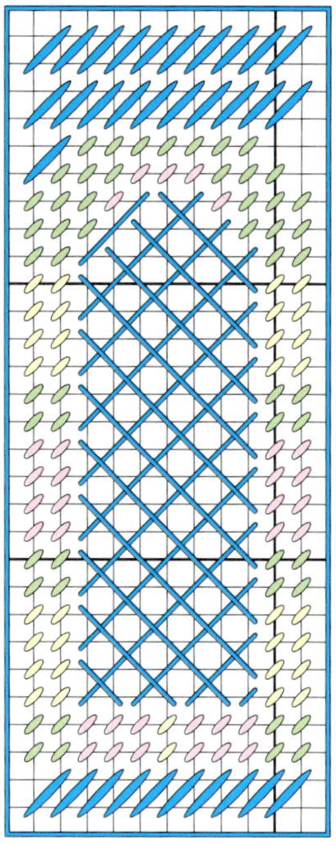

Flower Shoppe Bay Window Front
12 holes x 30 holes
Cut 1 from clear plastic canvas

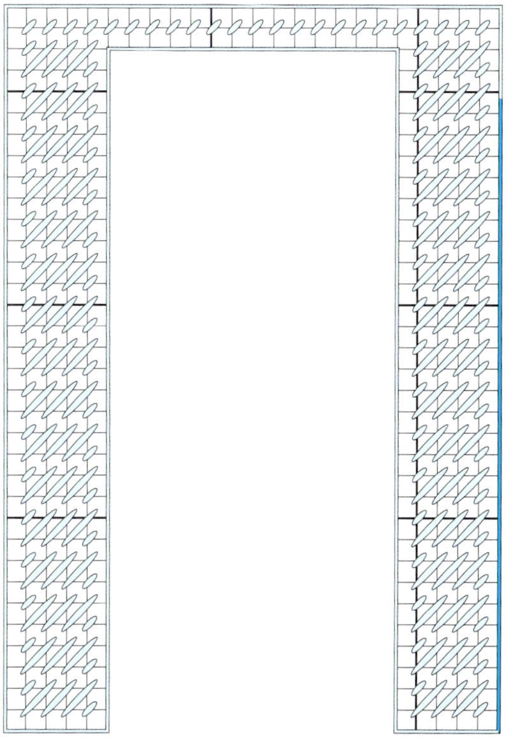

Flower Shoppe Left Side
24 holes x 34 holes
Cut 1 from clear plastic canvas

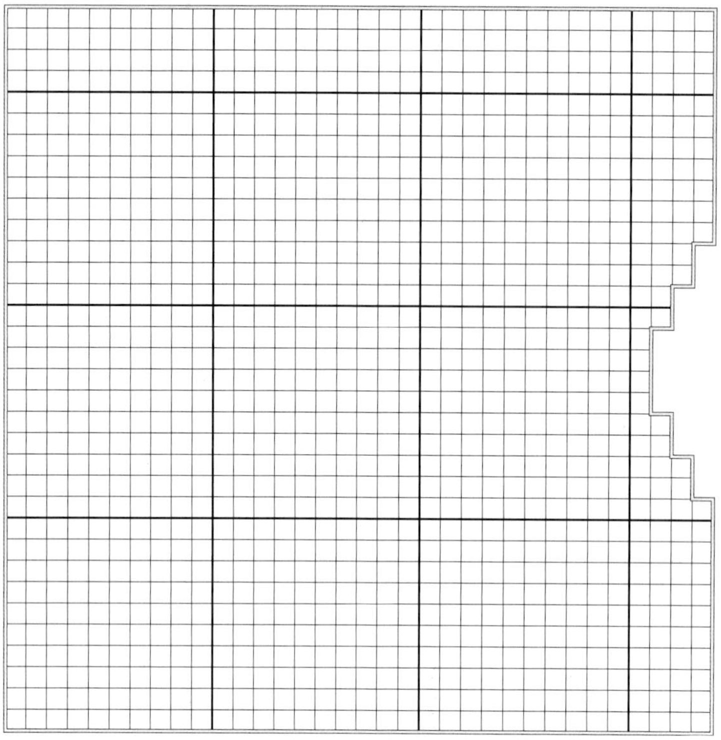

Flower Shoppe Support
34 holes x 34 holes
Cut 2 from clear plastic canvas;
leave unstitched

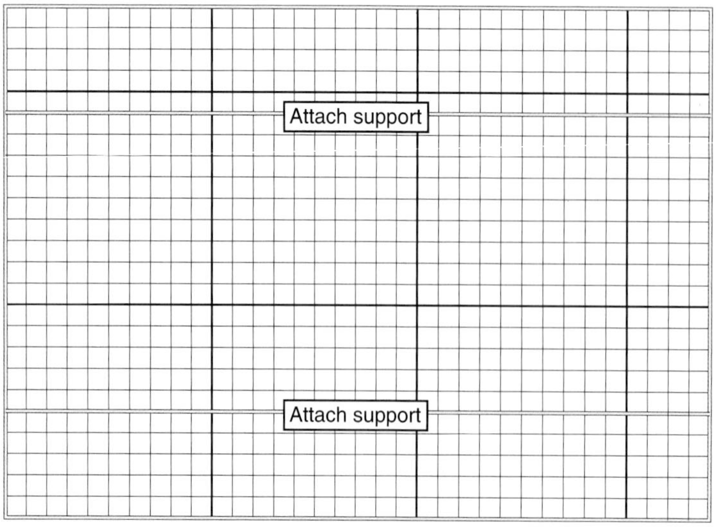

Flower Shoppe Bottom
34 holes x 24 holes
Cut 1 from clear plastic canvas;
leave unstitched

Saloon

Size: **Coaster Holder:** 5⅛ inches W x 7⅜ inches H x 5¼ inches D (13cm x 18.7cm x 13.3cm)
Coaster: 4¾ inches W x 4¾ inches H (12.1cm x 12.1cm)

Skill Level: Beginner

Materials

- ❑ 7-count plastic canvas:
  - 3 sheets clear
  - 1½ sheets light brown
- ❑ Worsted weight yarn as listed in color key
- ❑ #16 tapestry needle
- ❑ Hot-glue gun *or* clear-drying craft glue

Stitching Step by Step

Coaster Holder

1 Cut front, back, right and left sides, bottom, two supports, front roof, top roof and four posts from clear plastic canvas according to graphs.

2 Stitch plastic canvas according to graphs, filling in uncoded areas on all pieces *except* bottom piece with beige Continental Stitches. Supports will remain unstitched. Leave red line on saloon front unstitched; it will be used for attaching front roof later.

3 Using medium brown yarn through step 5, Overcast both short sides and one long side (front edge) of front roof. Whipstitch back edge of front roof to saloon front where indicated by red line on graph.

4 Whipstitch supports to left side and coaster holder bottom as described in directions for Assembly in the General Instructions, page 1. Overcast remaining edges of supports and top edge of opening in left side.

5 Whipstitch front, left side, back and right side together along corners. Whipstitch assembled walls to bottom with front wall adjacent to stitched area of bottom; Overcast bottom edge of opening in left side and edges adjacent to stitching on front of saloon bottom. Overcast all top edges. Tack supports to right and left sides to hold them securely.

6 Using dark brown yarn, Whipstitch posts together in pairs, wrong sides facing. Referring to photo throughout, glue bottoms of posts to stitched area of bottom, and tops of posts to underside of front roof.

7 Using medium brown yarn, Whipstitch top roof to top of saloon.

Coasters

1 Cut six coasters from clear plastic canvas and six coasters from light brown plastic canvas according to graph.

2 Stitch clear plastic canvas coasters according to graph, filling in uncoded areas with beige Continental Stitches. Light brown coasters will be used for backing and will remain unstitched.

3 Using beige yarn, Whipstitch a light brown coaster to the wrong side of each stitched coaster.

4 Insert coasters in coaster holder through slot in left side.

COLOR KEY

Yards	Worsted Weight Yarn
55 (50.3m)	Beige
54 (49.4m)	Medium brown
20 (18.3m)	Dark brown
15 (13.7m)	White
10 (9.1m)	Gray
7 (6.4m)	Light brown
2 (1.8m)	Black
	Uncoded areas on coasters and coaster holder are beige Continental Stitches

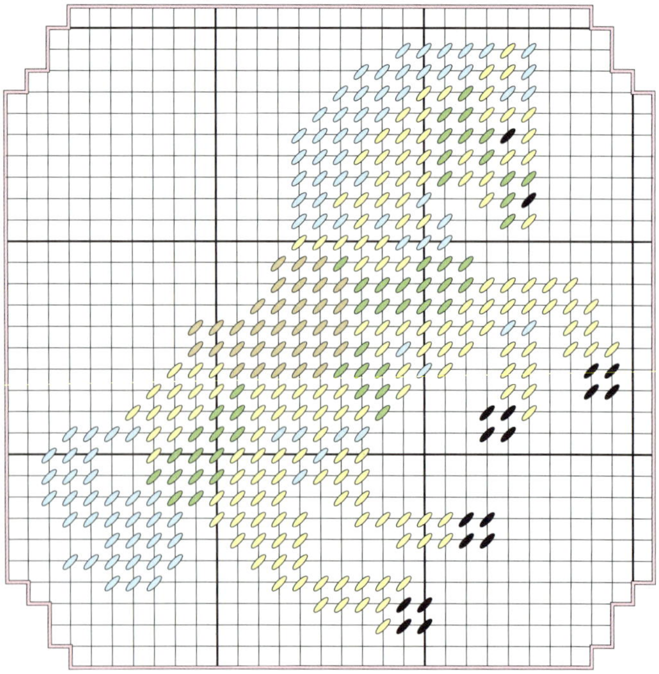

Saloon Coaster
31 holes x 31 holes
Cut 6 from clear plastic canvas;
stitch as shown
Cut 6 from light brown plastic canvas;
leave unstitched

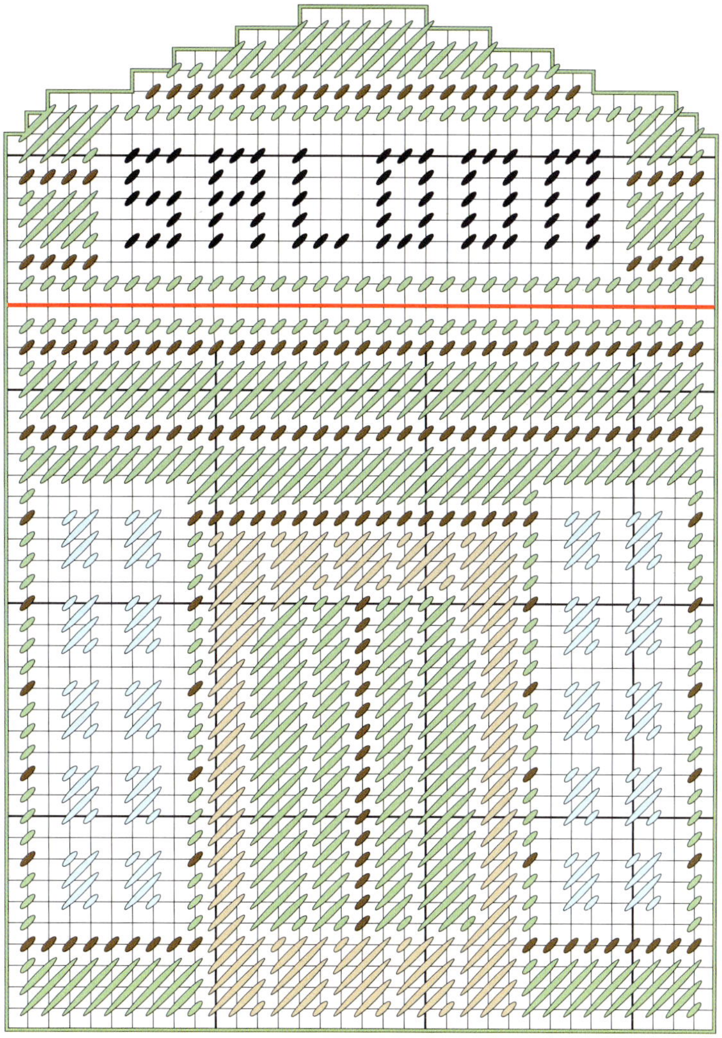

Saloon Front
34 holes x 48 holes
Cut 1 from clear plastic canvas

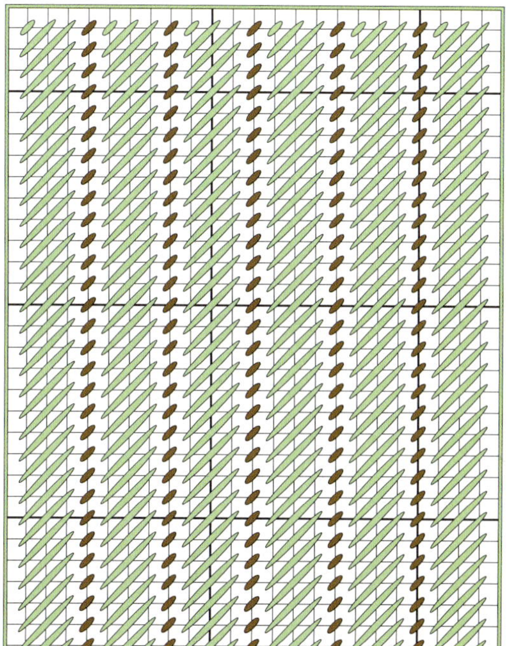

Saloon Right Side
24 holes x 34 holes
Cut 1 from clear plastic canvas

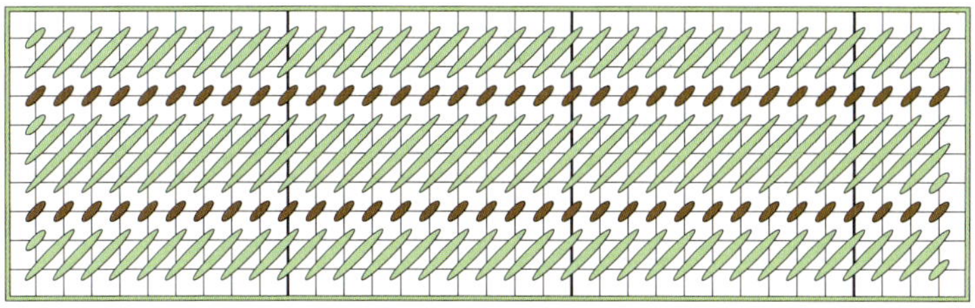

Saloon Front Roof
34 holes x 10 holes
Cut 1 from clear plastic canvas

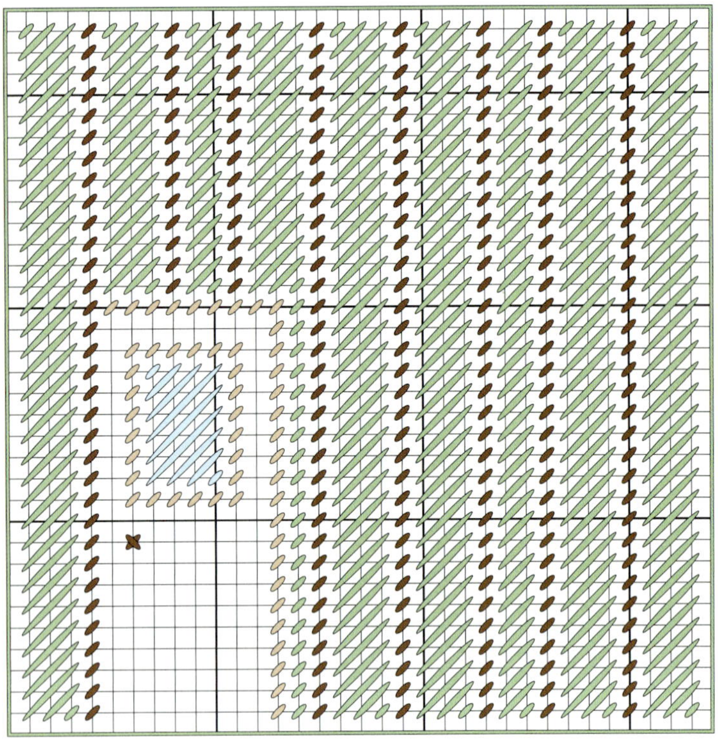

Saloon Back
34 holes x 34 holes
Cut 1 from clear plastic canvas

Saloon Left Side
24 holes x 34 holes
Cut 1 from clear plastic canvas

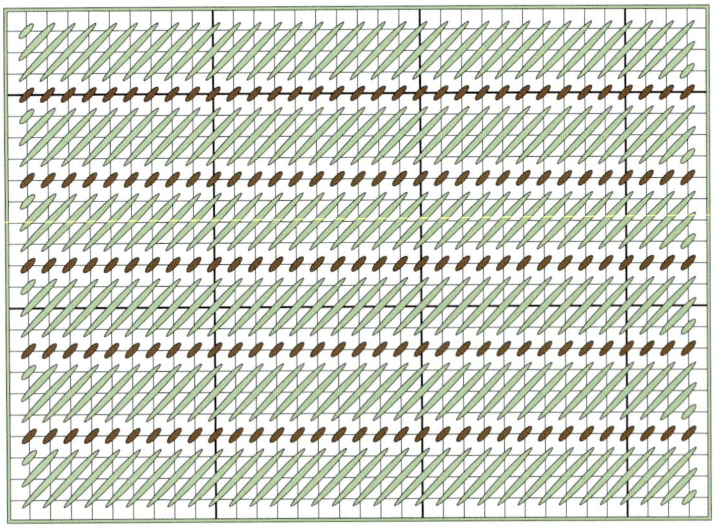

Saloon Top Roof
34 holes x 24 holes
Cut 1 from clear plastic canvas

COLOR KEY

Yards	Worsted Weight Yarn
55 (50.3m)	Beige
54 (49.4m)	Medium brown
20 (18.3m)	Dark brown
15 (13.7m)	White
10 (9.1m)	Gray
7 (6.4m)	Light brown
2 (1.8m)	Black
	Uncoded areas on coasters and coaster holder are beige Continental Stitches

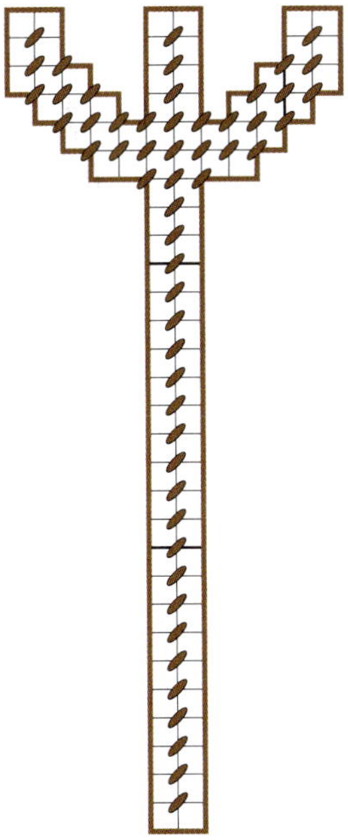

Saloon Post
12 holes x 29 holes
Cut 4 from clear plastic canvas

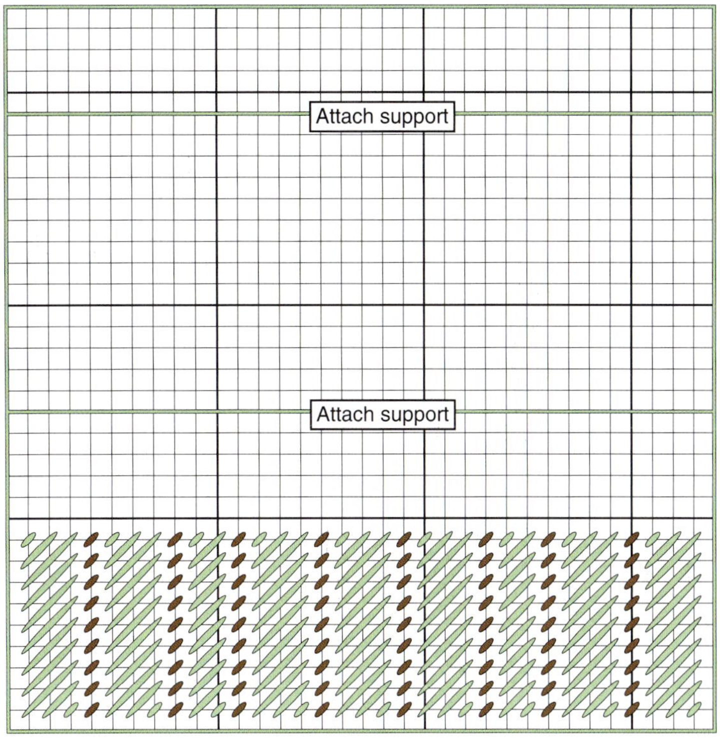

Saloon Bottom
34 holes x 34 holes
Cut 1 from clear plastic canvas

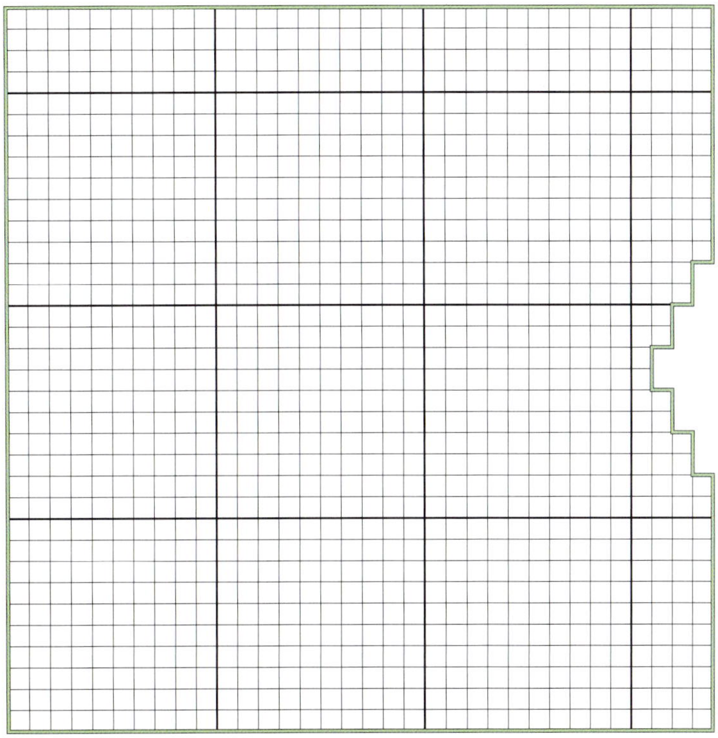

Saloon Support
34 holes x 34 holes
Cut 2 from clear plastic canvas;
leave unstitched

Coffee Shop

Size: **Coaster Holder:** $5\frac{3}{4}$ inches W x $7\frac{3}{8}$ inches H x $5\frac{1}{4}$ inches D (14.6cm x 18.7cm x 13.3cm)
Coaster: $4\frac{1}{2}$ inches W x $4\frac{1}{2}$ inches H (11.4cm x 11.4cm)

Skill Level: Beginner

Materials

- ❑ 7-count plastic canvas:
  - 3 sheets clear
  - $1\frac{1}{2}$ sheets pink
- ❑ Worsted weight yarn as listed in color key
- ❑ Metallic craft cord as listed in color key
- ❑ #16 tapestry needle
- ❑ Hot-glue gun *or* clear-drying craft glue

Stitching Step by Step

Coaster Holder

1 Cut front, back, right and left sides, bottom, two supports, two roofs, one awning front and two awning sides from clear plastic canvas according to graphs.

2 Stitch plastic canvas according to graphs, reversing one awning side before stitching. Supports and bottom will remain unstitched. Leave red line on front unstitched; it will be used for attaching awning later.

3 When background stitching is complete, Straight Stitch crosshatch pattern over windows on front, back and right side using 2 plies separated from a length of pink yarn.

4 Using light brown yarn throughout, Whipstitch supports to left side and coaster holder bottom as described in directions for Assembly in the General Instructions, page 1. Overcast remaining edges of supports and top edge of opening in left side.

5 Using white yarn through step 7, Whipstitch a straight edge of one awning side to one end of the awning front, with the diagonal edge of the awning side angling down and toward the back. In the same manner, Whipstitch the remaining awning side to the other end of the awning front.

6 Overcast remaining edges of awning sides and front edge of awning front.

7 Whipstitch back edge of awning front to coaster holder front where indicated by red line on graph.

8 Using light brown yarn throughout, Whipstitch front, left side, back and right side together along corners. Whipstitch assembled walls to unstitched bottom, Overcasting bottom edge of opening in left side. Overcast all top edges. Tack supports to right and left sides to hold them securely.

9 Using rose yarn, Whipstitch roof pieces together along one long edge. Overcast remaining edges.

10 Glue roof to coffee shop; glue back (diagonal) edges of awning sides to front of coffee shop.

Coasters

1 Cut six coasters from clear plastic canvas and six coasters from pink plastic canvas according to graph.

2 Stitch clear plastic canvas coasters according to graph, filling in uncoded areas with pink Continental Stitches. Pink coasters will be used for backing and will remain unstitched.

3 When background stitching is complete, Backstitch cup and saucer using 2 plies separated from a length of dark brown yarn.

4 Using pink yarn, Whipstitch a pink coaster to the wrong side of each stitched coaster.

5 Insert coasters in coaster holder through slot in left side.

COLOR KEY

Yards	Worsted Weight Yarn
47 (43m)	Pink
33 (30.2m)	Light brown
21 (19.2m)	White
21 (19.2m)	Medium brown
3 (2.7m)	Dark rose
10 (9.1m)	Rose
8 (7.3m)	Dark brown
2 (1.8m)	Dark olive
	Uncoded areas on coasters are pink Continental Stitches
	Pink 2-ply Straight Stitch
	Dark brown 2-ply Backstitch
	Metallic Craft Cord
8 (7.3m)	Gold

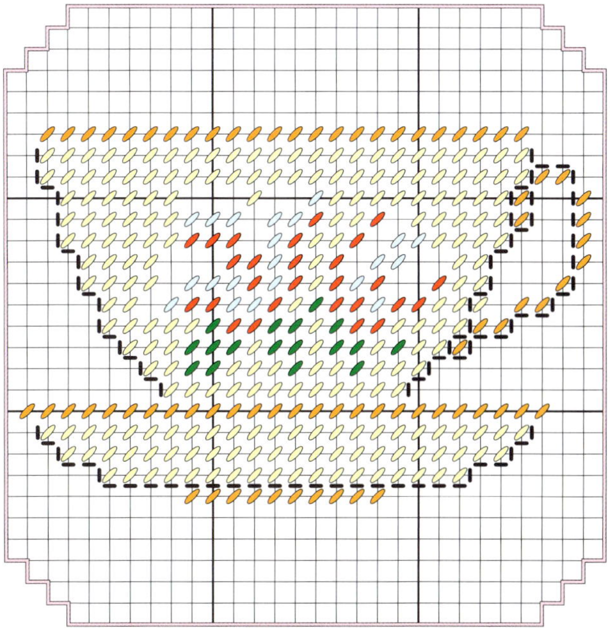

Coffee Shop Coaster
29 holes x 29 holes
Cut 6 from clear plastic canvas;
stitch as shown
Cut 6 from pink plastic canvas;
leave unstitched

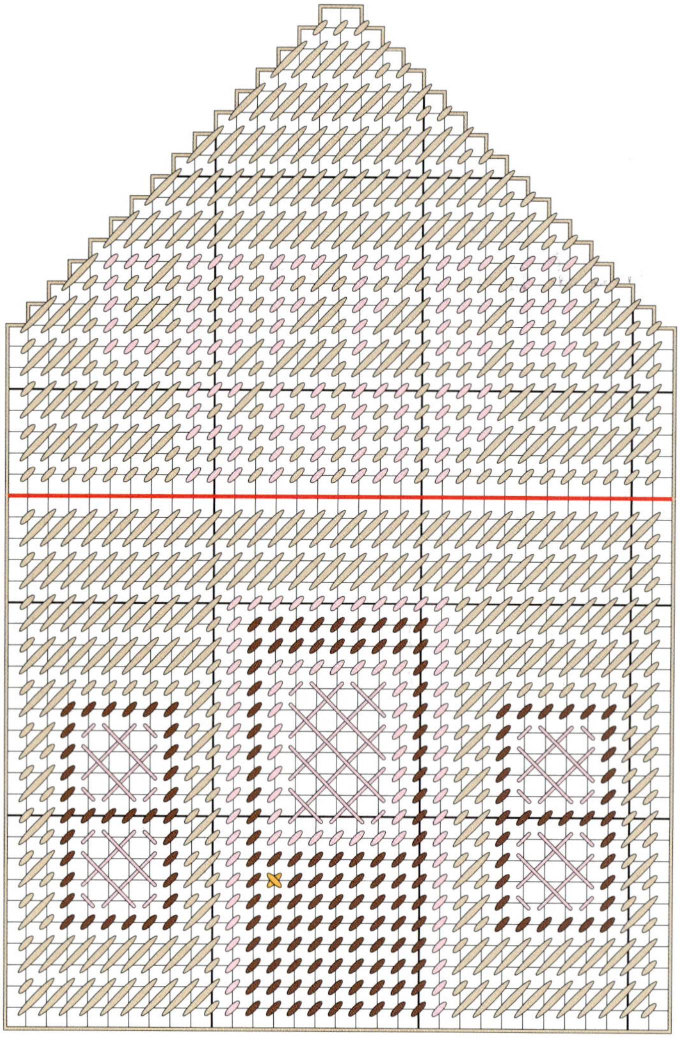

Coffee Shop Front
32 holes x 48 holes
Cut 1 from clear plastic canvas

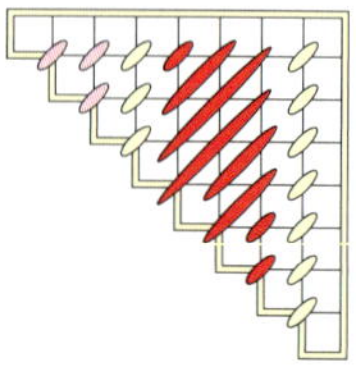

Coffee Shop Awning Side
8 holes x 8 holes
Cut 2 from clear plastic canvas; reverse 1 before stitching

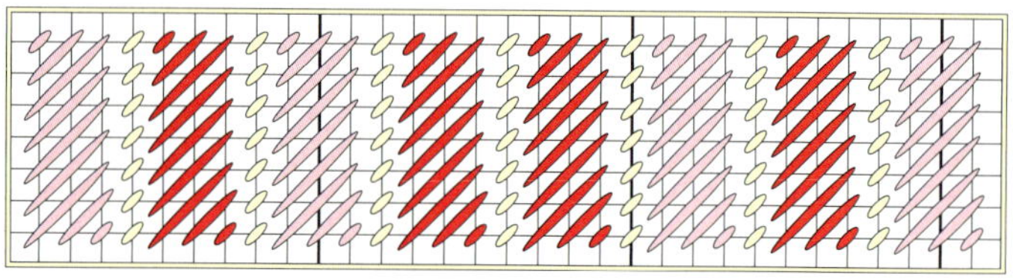

Coffee Shop Awning Front
32 holes x 8 holes
Cut 1 from clear plastic canvas

COLOR KEY

Yards	Worsted Weight Yarn
47 (43m)	Pink
33 (30.2m)	Light brown
21 (19.2m)	White
21 (19.2m)	Medium brown
3 (2.7m)	Dark rose
10 (9.1m)	Rose
8 (7.3m)	Dark brown
2 (1.8m)	Dark olive
	Uncoded areas on coasters are pink Continental Stitches
	Pink 2-ply Straight Stitch
	Dark brown 2-ply Backstitch
	Metallic Craft Cord
8 (7.3m)	Gold

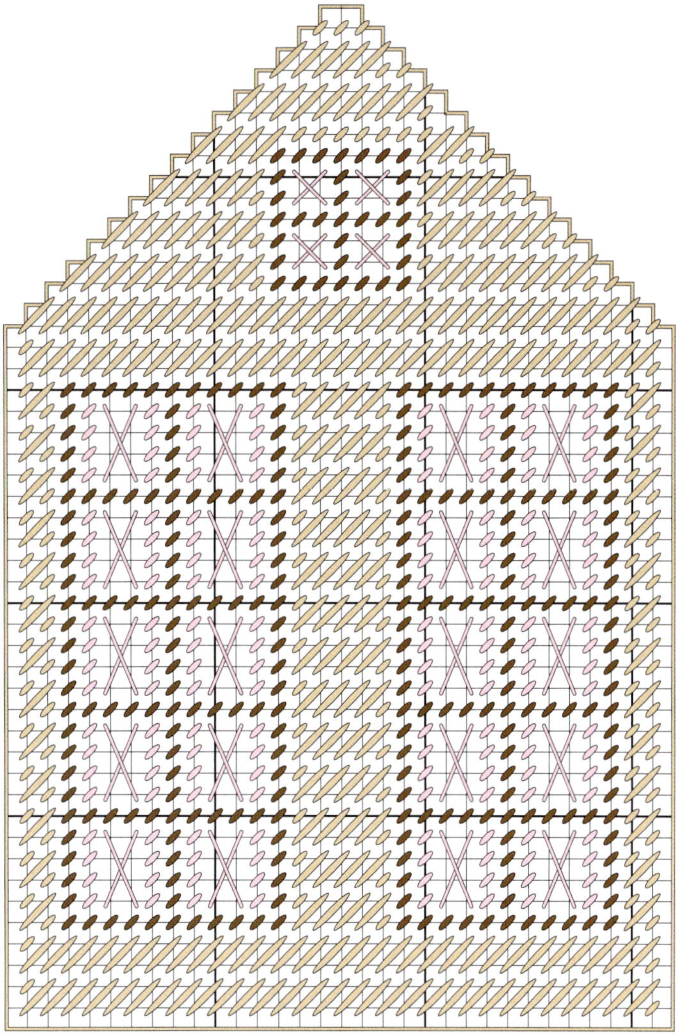

Coffee Shop Back
32 holes x 48 holes
Cut 1 from clear plastic canvas

Coffee Shop Roof
30 holes x 26 holes
Cut 2 from clear plastic canvas

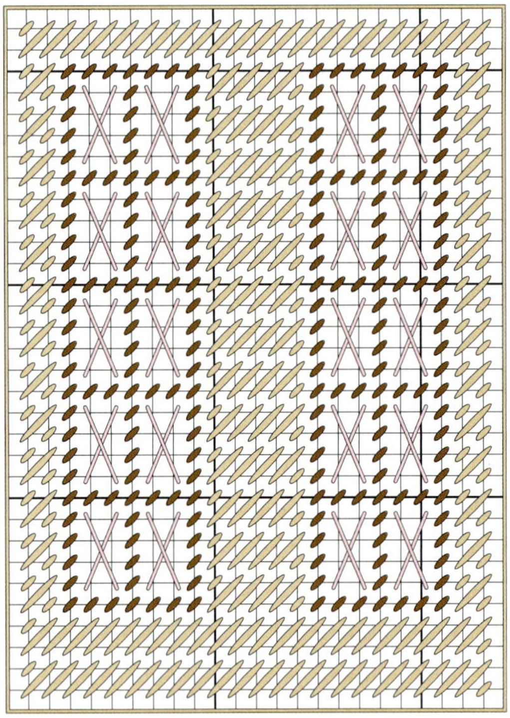

Coffee Shop Right Side
24 holes x 33 holes
Cut 1 from clear plastic canvas

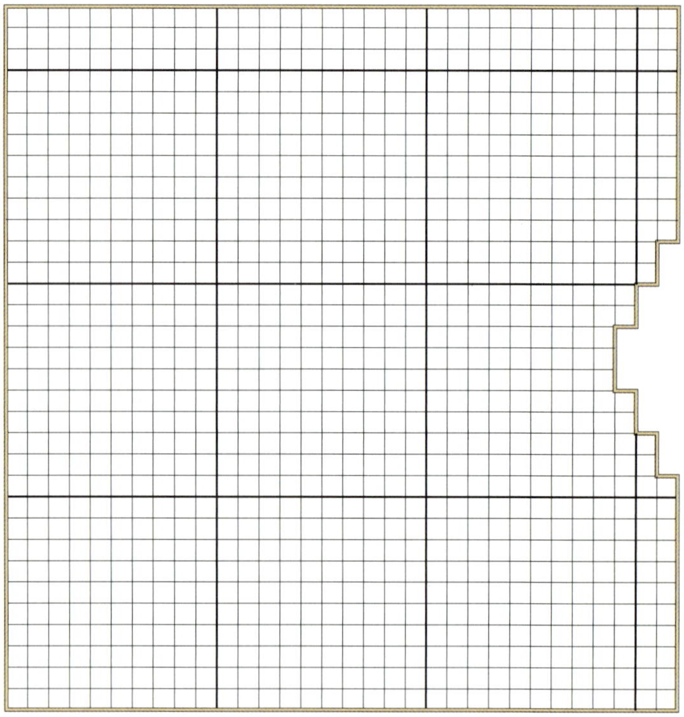

Coffee Shop Support
32 holes x 33 holes
Cut 2 from clear plastic canvas;
leave unstitched

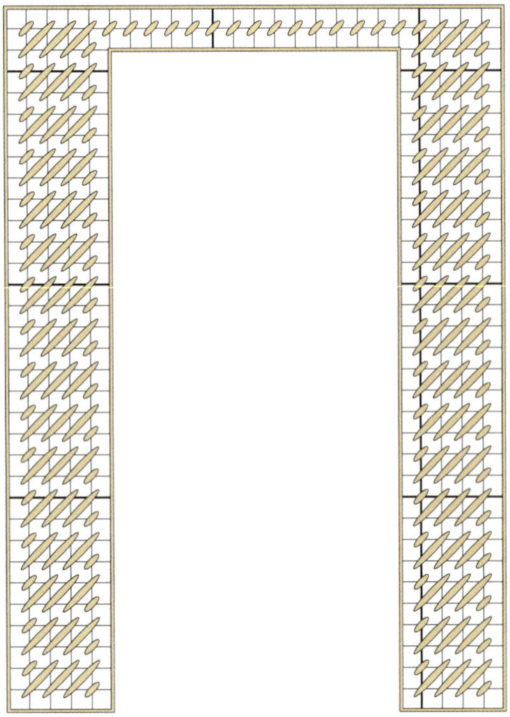

Coffee Shop Left Side
24 holes x 33 holes
Cut 1 from clear plastic canvas

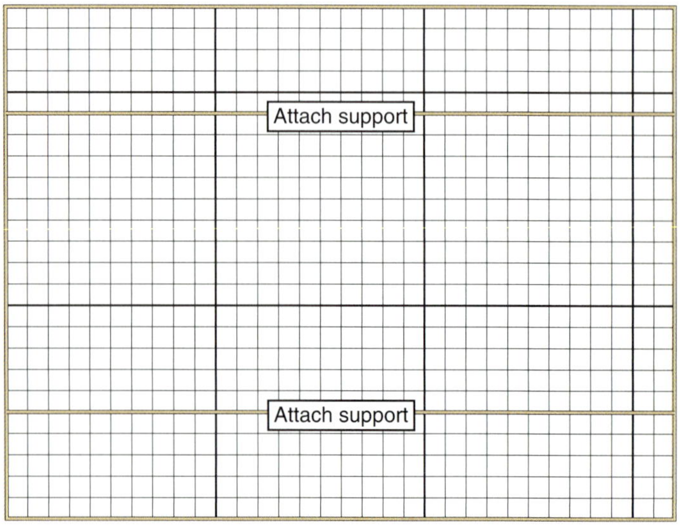

Coffee Shop Bottom
32 holes x 24 holes
Cut 1 from clear plastic canvas;
leave unstitched

Garage

Size: **Coaster Holder:** 5½ inches W x 5⅛ inches H x 4½ inches D (14cm x 13cm x 11.4cm)
Coaster: 4⅞ inches W x 4⅝ inches H (12.4cm x 11.8cm)

Skill Level: Beginner

Materials

- ❑ 7-count plastic canvas:
  - 3 sheets clear
  - 1½ sheets white
- ❑ Worsted weight yarn as listed in color key
- ❑ Metallic craft cord as listed in color key
- ❑ #16 tapestry needle
- ❑ Hot-glue gun *or* clear-drying craft glue

Stitching Step by Step

Coaster Holder

1 Cut front, back, right and left sides, bottom, two supports, roof, garage overhang front, two garage overhang top/bottom pieces and two garage overhang sides from clear plastic canvas according to graphs.

2 Stitch plastic canvas according to graphs, leaving unstitched area on front according to graph. Supports and bottom will remain unstitched. Leave red line on front unstitched; it will be used for attaching overhang later.

3 Using gray yarn, Whipstitch supports to left side and coaster holder bottom as described in directions for Assembly in the General Instructions, page 1. Overcast remaining edges of supports and top edge of opening in left side.

4 Using brick yarn, Whipstitch overhang top to overhang front along one long edge; Whipstitch overhang bottom to other long edge of overhang front. Whipstitch overhang sides to ends of overhang.

5 Using gray yarn through step 7 and referring to photo, Whipstitch unstitched back edge of overhang bottom to front where indicated by horizontal red Whipstitching line on graph.

6 Whipstitch front, left side, back and right side together along corners, stitching through all three layers at top of front wall to attach side edges of assembled overhang. Whipstitch assembled walls to unstitched bottom, Overcasting bottom edge of opening in left side. Overcast all top edges. Tack supports to right and left sides to hold them securely.

7 Whipstitch roof to garage's top edges, stitching through all three layers on front edge to attach top of overhang.

Coasters

1 Cut six coasters from clear plastic canvas and six coasters from white plastic canvas according to graph.

2 Stitch clear plastic canvas coasters according to graph, filling in uncoded areas with white Continental Stitches. White coasters will be used for backing and will remain unstitched.

3 Using white yarn, Whipstitch a white coaster to the wrong side of each stitched coaster.

4 Insert coasters in coaster holder through slot in left side.

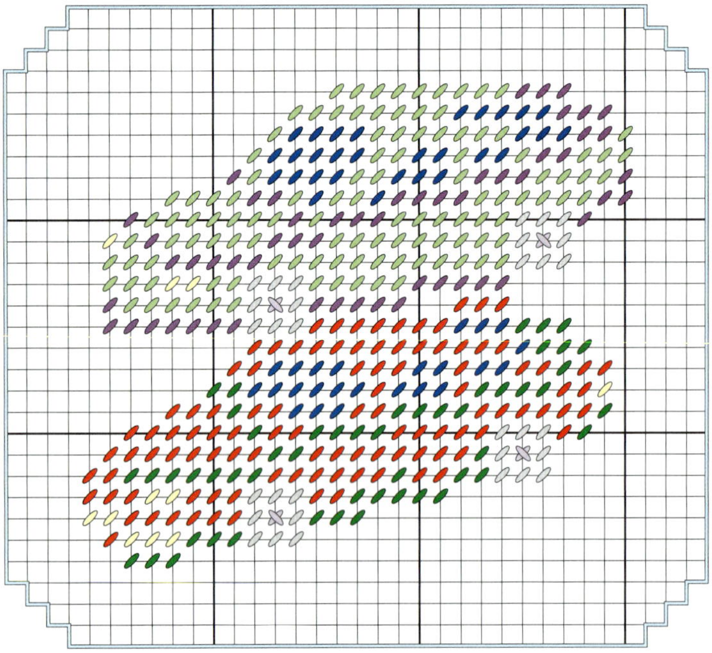

Garage Coaster
34 holes x 30 holes
Cut 6 from clear plastic canvas;
stitch as shown
Cut 6 from white plastic canvas;
leave unstitched

COLOR KEY	
Yards	**Worsted Weight Yarn**
54 (49.4m)	White
44 (40.2m)	Gray
16 (14.6m)	Brick
11 (10.1m)	Medium green
9 (8.2m)	Red
5 (4.6m)	Dark green
5 (4.6m)	Dark red
3 (2.7m)	Very dark gray
	Uncoded areas on coasters are white Continental Stitches
	Metallic Craft Cord
2 (1.8m)	Gold
2 (1.8m)	Silver

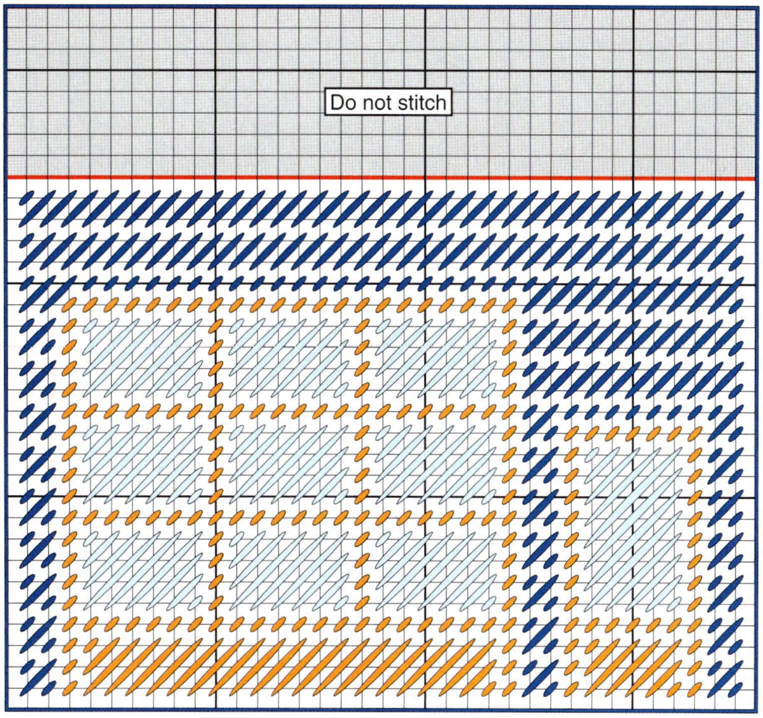

Garage Front
36 holes x 33 holes
Cut 1 from clear plastic canvas

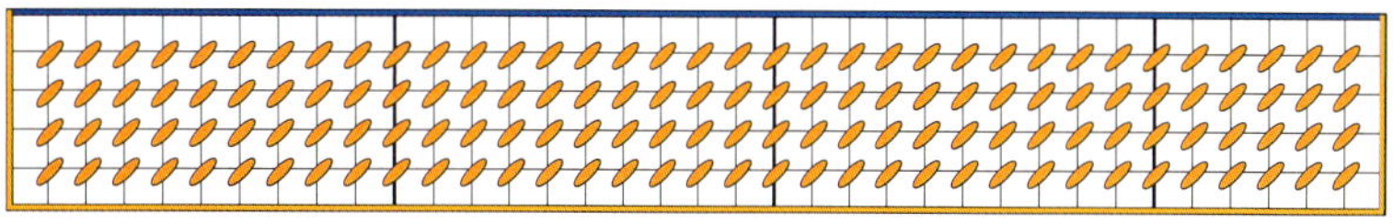

Garage Overhang Top/Bottom
36 holes x 5 holes
Cut 2 from clear plastic canvas

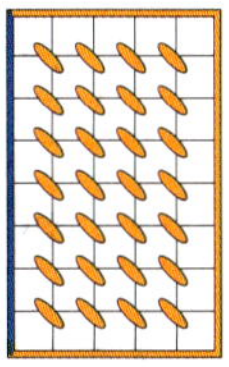

Garage Overhang Side
5 holes x 8 holes
Cut 2 from clear plastic canvas

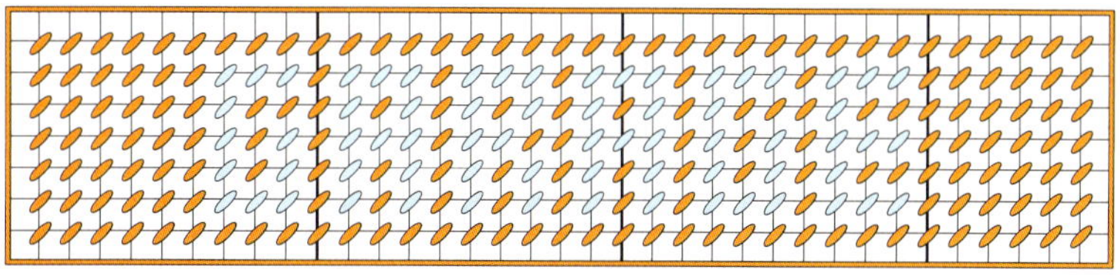

Garage Overhang Front
36 holes x 8 holes
Cut 1 from clear plastic canvas

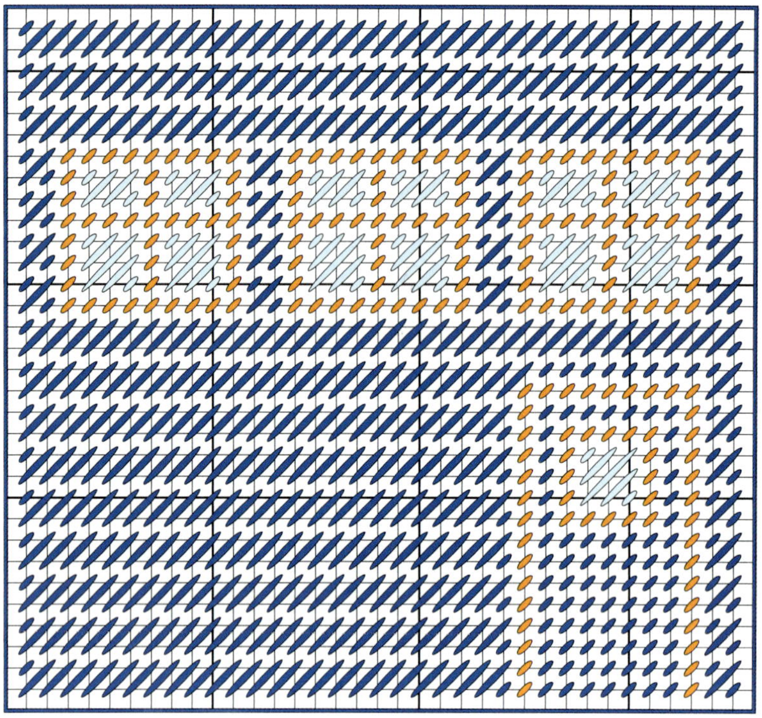

Garage Back
36 holes x 33 holes
Cut 1 from clear plastic canvas

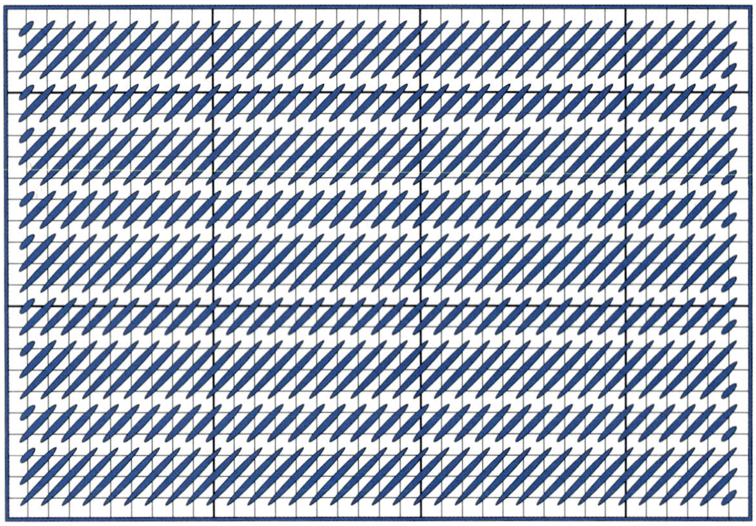

Garage Roof
36 holes x 24 holes
Cut 1 from clear plastic canvas

COLOR KEY

Yards	Worsted Weight Yarn
54 (49.4m)	White
44 (40.2m)	Gray
16 (14.6m)	Brick
11 (10.1m)	Medium green
9 (8.2m)	Red
5 (4.6m)	Dark green
5 (4.6m)	Dark red
3 (2.7m)	Very dark gray
	Uncoded areas on coasters are white Continental Stitches
	Metallic Craft Cord
2 (1.8m)	Gold
2 (1.8m)	Silver

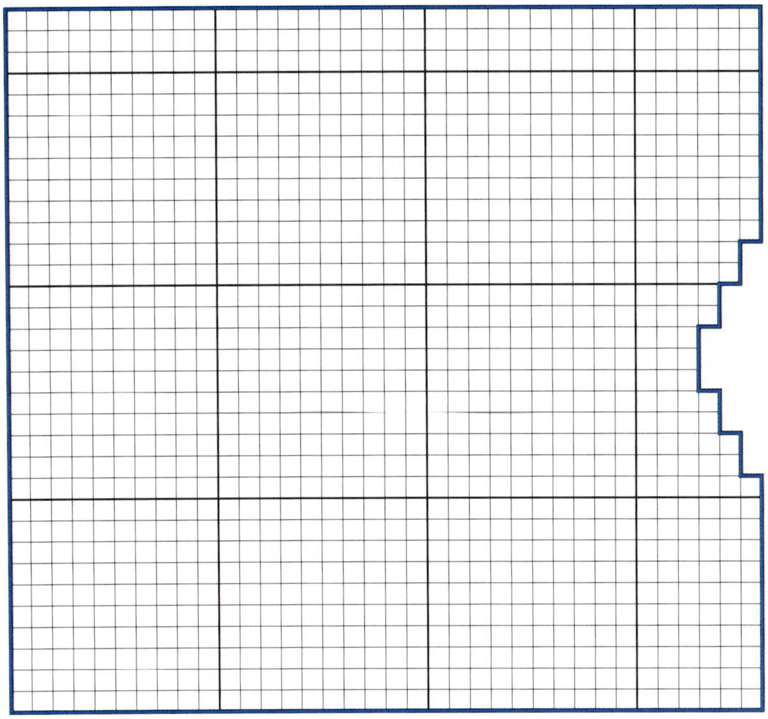

Garage Support
36 holes x 33 holes
Cut 2 from clear plastic canvas;
leave unstitched

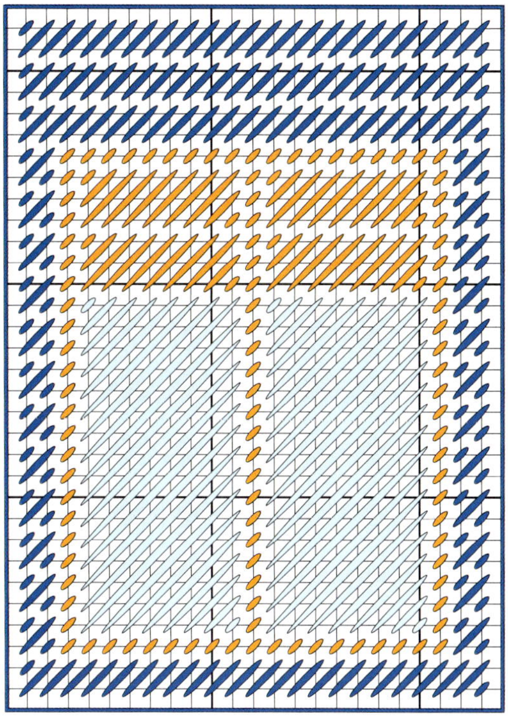

Garage Right Side
24 holes x 33 holes
Cut 1 from clear plastic canvas

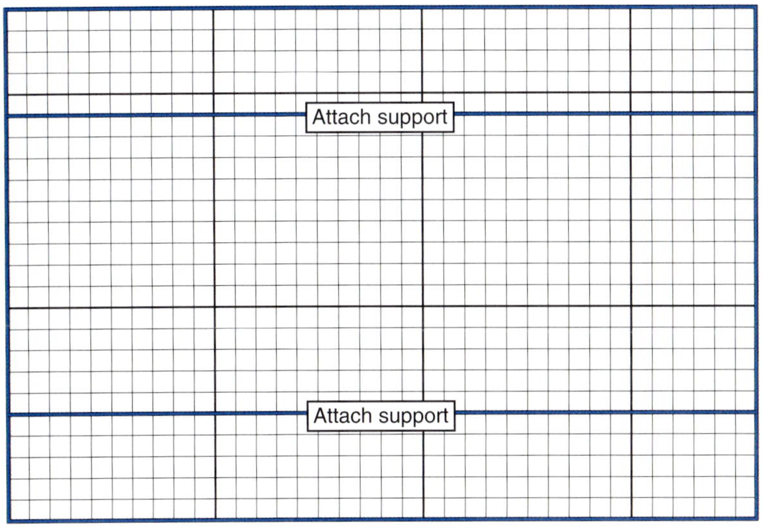

Garage Bottom
36 holes x 24 holes
Cut 1 from clear plastic canvas;
leave unstitched

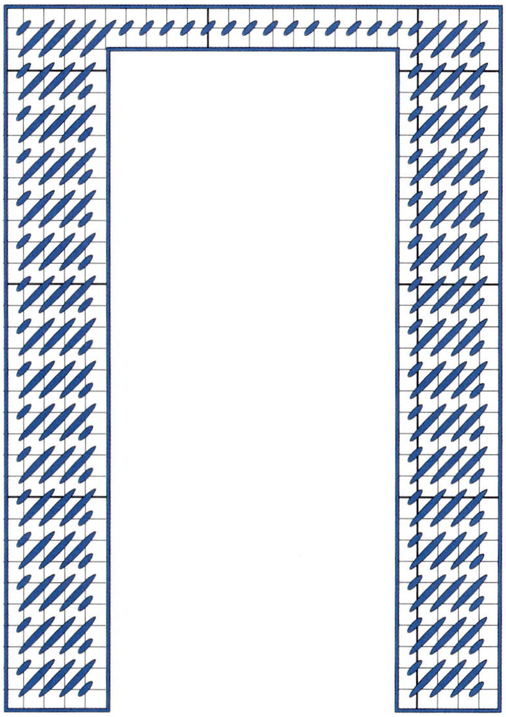

Garage Left Side
24 holes x 33 holes
Cut 1 from clear plastic canvas

306 E. Parr Road
Berne, IN 46711
NeedlecraftShop.com

The full line of The Needlecraft Shop products is carried by Annie's Attic catalog.

TOLL-FREE ORDER LINE
or to request a free catalog
(800) 582-6643
Customer Service
(800) 449-0440
Fax (800) 882-6643
Visit www.AnniesAttic.com

ISBN-10: 1-57367-242-4
ISBN-13: 978-1-57367-242-9

Printed in USA
1 2 3 4 5 6 7 8 9

Shopping for Supplies

For supplies, first shop your local craft and needlework stores. Some supplies may be found in fabric, hardware and discount stores. If you are unable to find the supplies you need, please call Annie's Attic at (800) 259-4000 to request a free catalog that sells plastic canvas supplies.

Getting Started

Before You Cut

Buy one brand of canvas for each entire project, as brands can differ slightly in the distance between bars. Count holes carefully from the graph before you cut, using the bolder lines that show each 10 holes. These 10-mesh lines begin in the lower left corner of each graph to make counting easier. Mark canvas before cutting, then remove all marks completely before stitching. If the piece is cut in a rectangular or square shape and is either not worked, or worked with only one color and one type of stitch, we do not include the graph in the pattern. Instead, we give the cutting and stitching instructions in the general instructions or with the individual project instructions.

Covering the Canvas

Bring needle up from back of work, leaving a short length of yarn on back of canvas; work over short length to secure. To end a thread, weave needle and thread through the wrong side of your last few stitches; clip. Follow the numbers on the small graphs beside each stitch illustration; bring your needle up from the back of the work on odd numbers and down through the front of the work on even numbers. Work embroidery stitches last, after the canvas has been completely covered by the needlepoint stitches.

Basic Stitches

Continental

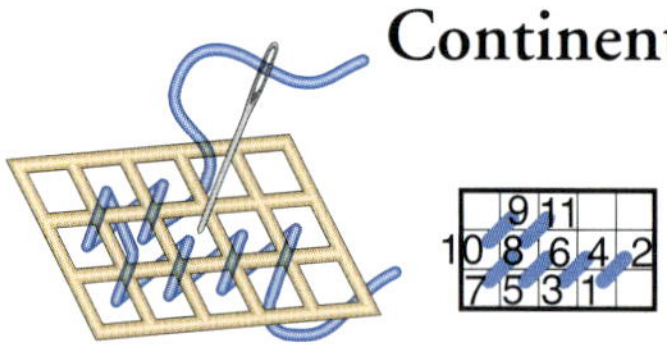

Overcast

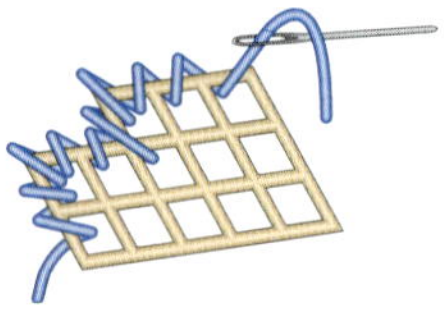

Whipstitch

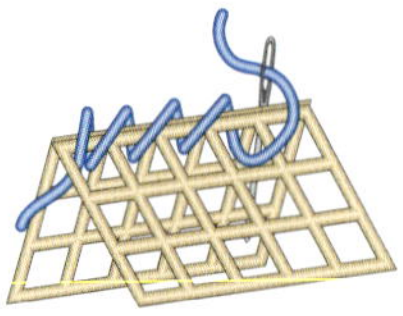

Slanted Gobelin

Long

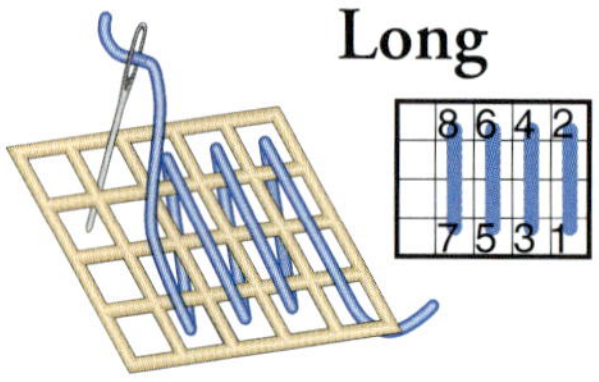

Cross

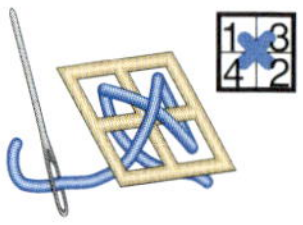

Embroidery Stitches

French Knot

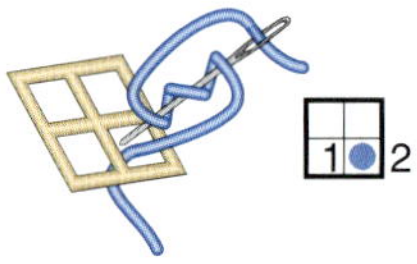

Lazy Daisy

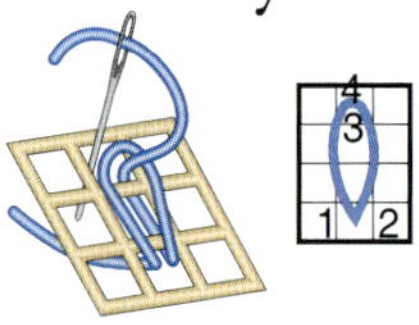

Backstitch

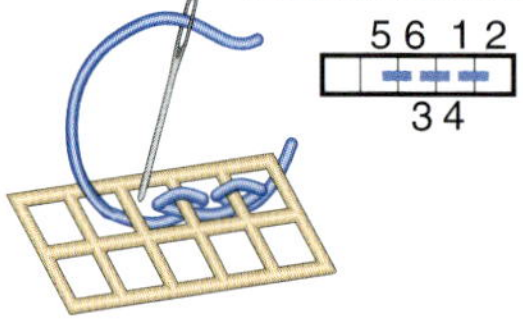

Straight

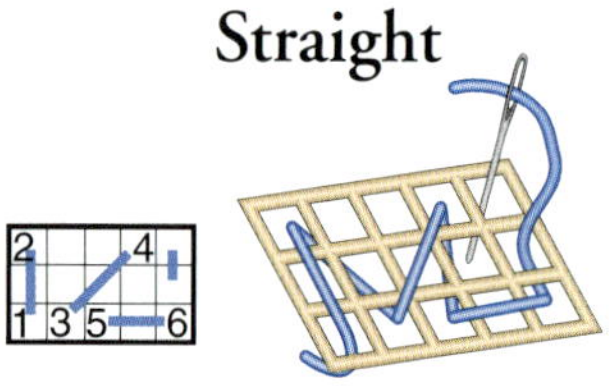

METRIC KEY:
millimeters = (mm)
centimeters = (cm)
meters = (m)
grams = (g)